MW01488761

PK

A Preacher's Kid Comes of Age in the Great Depression And World War II

By Bob Haslam

TABLE OF CONTENTS

—⟨∾⟩—

Dedication/Introduction

———

This book was written because of my beloved wife Fran's urging. To her I offer my deep gratitude for endless reading and editing of the manuscript and offering valuable suggestions.

I dedicate this book to my grandchildren and that first great grandson. I love you all dearly, and hope that this rehearsal of my growing-up years will interest you and be of value to your lives.

My story relates to a wide audience due to the depressed economy of the present, as well as the fact that we are involved in a time of war. Come with me to hear tales of my nomadic life as a preacher's kid during the Great Depression and World War II in Western Washington State. You will find amazing correlations between the era I describe and the one in which we now live.

My growing-up years were difficult but good. The Great Depression and World War II were "times that try men's souls." I salute my parents who carried our family through those troubling years. I honor them for the moral and spiritual formation they fostered in me.

CHAPTER ONE
My Birth May Have Caused the Great Depression

—⚡—

Bobby as a toddler

Having a ball

Bathing beauty

Lillian, my other mother

My first house in Seattle at 18 W. Dravas Street

Sitting on top of the world

"Before I formed you in the womb I knew you,
before you were born I set you apart."
(Jeremiah 1:5)

SURPRISE, SURPRISE!

I really wasn't expecting it, but on Mother's Day, May 13, 1928, I emerged from my mother's womb and took my first breath—followed by the loudest crying you ever heard. Yes, I had ten fingers and ten toes, two ears and a nose—and very healthy lungs. Until my mother's death, every year on Mother's Day she reminded me that I was the best Mother's Day gift she ever received. I can imagine that on some of my ornery growing-up days, she might have questioned that thought.

My parents' names were Rev. Oliver and Rachel Becraft Haslam. I honor their memory as they courageously guided their four children through the austere years of the Great Depression and World War II.

My birth in St. Luke's Hospital in Seattle, Washington, in 1928 had serious repercussions. Seventeen months later, the stock market crash of 1929 took place. Apparently, there was one too many mouths to feed, and the country's economy couldn't handle it. And just maybe my Dad couldn't afford to pay the hospital bill. Perhaps for that reason St. Luke's Hospital went belly up. It no longer exists, and it's possibly all my fault.

I was a Depression baby. My story of growing up during the long years of the Great Depression in a preacher's home is a story of family survival during tough times.

MY FIRST TWO YEARS

I don't remember a whole lot about my first two years at 18 West Dravus Street in Seattle at the bottom of the north slope of Queen Ann Hill. My parents served as missionaries in Japan before I was born, and when they came back to the U.S., Dad pastored a church in Auburn, WA, where my sister, Irene, was born.

Dad established a Japanese church in Seattle among the large Asian population. For two years he held services in rented facilities downtown on Sunday mornings with a small Japanese congregation. On Sunday evenings they carried me as an infant kicking and screaming into Seattle First Church down the block from our house across Third Avenue West from Seattle Pacific College, now Seattle Pacific University.

When the Japanese church venture did not work out, Dad made himself available for appointment to a church. He said, "I'm a missionary, so feel free to send me wherever you see fit." And they did just that—appointed him, with his wife and four children to a church without a parsonage. The meager pastor's income was inadequate to rent a house.

CHAPTER TWO
The Town Shut Down, People Came Together

The Church in National: Ed, Lilian,
Bobby, and Irene

The house Dad built: Irene, Bobby, Ed, and Lilian

Bundled up for winter play

*"Let the little children come to me,
and do not hinder them,
for the kingdom of heaven
belongs to such as these."*
(Matthew 19:14)

NATIONAL CONCERNS

W hen I was two years old, my father was appointed to pastor the only church in National, Washington, nestled near the base of Mount Rainier. It was a Weyerhaeuser lumber company town. Everyone in town worked in the lumber industry that included logging in the forest and the town's lumber mill. All the houses were prefabricated, unpainted buildings located along plank roads made of 4x4 lumber slabs that rumbled like thunder when cars drove over them.

My folks had four children ranging in age from two to thirteen, and no place to live. Dad went to the Weyerhaeuser company office, told them his dilemma, and made a proposition. If the company would donate the lumber, my dad would build a new parsonage next to the church. Weyerhaeuser agreed and supplied enough third-grade lumber filled with holes where the knots had fallen out. We called it our "naughty pine" house.

Dad and my brother Ed, ten years old, built the house, and we moved in. Winds blew through the house through the open knotholes. Only later was wallpaper added on the inside and siding on the outside, but we had a roof over our heads. That updated house is still occupied to this day. As the effects of the Depression deepened, building stopped and the lumber mill shut down, along with logging operations. There we were, all the church people out of work and no jobs available.

Then came "relief tickets," as we called them then, the 1930s version of food stamps. When the offering plates were passed, there were only a few coins in it. But members of the church knew the pastor had six mouths to feed, so they put relief tickets in the offering plate as their form of tithes and offerings. Dad took those to the company store that was still open and exchanged them for food.

Dad occasionally drove in his Model T Ford to Tacoma or Seattle where he obtained used clothing from the Good Will Store. Mother altered them to fit her growing brood of children. The ladies of the church held quilting bees, and our family and others made it through cold winter nights snugly tucked in under the quilts they made.

DEER ME
Fresh meat was scarce, and only seldom did we have any. A member of the church came to our house with a few venison steaks and roasts. When Dad asked him where he got the meat, the man's face turned red and he replied that he shot a deer out of season. He felt he had to do that to feed his wife and children, and he wanted to share it with his pastor's family.

Dad put his arm around the man's shoulders and said, "I don't condemn you for what you did. I know it was necessary. I don't feel I can accept the meat, and suggest you share it with others who are in greater need than we are." Dad's diplomacy paid off.

HILARIOUS HAPPENING
I told you about the third-grade lumber with holes in it. That applied to the ceilings as well. This led to one of the most humorous episodes in the National parsonage. Friends drove up from the city to our town for church, then drove on up to Mount Rainier. After church, Mother invited them for Sunday dinner, since they were friends and there were no restaurants in our small town.

While Mom cooked dinner, our company was in the living room. We were visiting with them when—*Plop!* A baby mouse fell through a hole in the ceiling into the lap of a woman who was sitting in a rocking chair. As she shrieked in horror, another baby mouse fell into her lap. She leaped from the rocking chair in a great fright.

Everyone in the room laughed hysterically as baby mice continued to tumble into the chair. Mama mouse had chosen the wrong spot to give birth to her babies. Our parsonage became known as "The Holey Place."

POINT *OH MY!*

Mount Rainier on the Paradise side was a popular destination for visitors from Seattle and Tacoma. We lived close to the national park entrance. When friends made the trip, they often stopped to visit on their way. Sometimes I was invited to go with them to Longmire and Paradise, then they dropped me off on their way home.

Driving to the mountain involved many twists and turns in the winding highway among the rocks and towering trees. A mountain stream wound its way among the foothills, which the highway followed. Occasionally, the top of the mountain could be seen between lower hills, but the real excitement came later. At one bend in the road the entire gorgeous mountain suddenly came into view. People would exclaim, *"Oh my!"* as they saw the snow-capped mountain in all its glory. We nicknamed that turn in the road, *"Point Oh My!"*

FAMILY FARM

With everyone out of work, how do you survive? We ended up with a family farm. Dad, with help from us kids, created a world-class garden each year with many kinds of vegetables. And in our shack out back we raised rabbits, as well as chickens that produced eggs (and chicken dinners). We built a pen and raised pigs that were put to rest and canned for winter meat, plus smoked hams and bacon.

The farmer across the highway, a member of our church, assigned a cow to my father, which we named Betsy. He milked her morning and evening. We had milk, cream, and made our own butter. I began the process of pushing the handle up and down on the butter churn that was filled with milk. When it began to thicken and I could no longer keep it going, an older brother or sister took over. We produced butter enough to share with others.

APRIL 8
Each year our cow was bred, and in due time a calf was born. We kids treated the calf like a pet and gave it a name. One year we couldn't agree on a name. Dad gave us one more day to agree or he would name the calf himself. When we failed to agree, Dad came up with the name. "Our calf was born on April 8, so that will be his name." To this day on April 8 I remember our much-loved calf and how he got his name.

Our beloved pets gave their lives so my mother could can the veal, along with pork, vegetables, and berries that we picked in the woods and on the hillsides. We were in the Great Depression and these were the only ways we could survive. My mother canned upwards of a thousand quarts of all kinds of meat, vegetables and fruit for the winter months.

PICKING FOR PROFIT
I mentioned picking fruit and canning it. In one day my dad and brother, along with another father and son, picked sixteen gallons of juicy, wild blackberries on the hillside across the highway from us. What a bonanza! We also picked wild red raspberries, black raspberries, huckleberries, and salmon berries.

One time my sister, Irene, and I took a bucket and went into the woods and filled it with blackberries. Unannounced, city friends dropped in on their way to or from the mountain. When we walked in with the bucket of freshly-picked blackberries, they offered to buy them. We agreed, so they gave us a handful of coins in payment.

Irene was already a schoolgirl, though I was still preschool age. She knew how to count and divided up the money between us. When I saw her pile of coins and mine, I complained. I had little coins (dimes) and she had bigger ones (nickels). I thought she was cheating by taking the bigger coins and complained to Dad. He grinned and gave me my first lesson in economics. He explained that the little coins were worth twice as much as the larger ones, so she needed to have more of them. I still wasn't convinced. My sister was happy to take my dimes and give me nickels in exchange.

POUND PARTIES

During the Depression, people shared what they had with one another. Once in a while, without notice, the entire church family showed up at the parsonage on an evening for a "pounding." They brought pounds of sugar, flour and other staples, vegetables, fruit, and—best of all—cakes and pies. My father kidded the congregation by telling them they ate all the cakes and pies before they went home.

Those were joyous occasions. Everyone was in a festive mood as they brought food supplies to the pastor and his family. The younger kids went outside and played games, sometimes in the dark. We Haslams knew we were loved and appreciated by our church family. Should I say it here? *During those difficult years, we never missed a meal!*

Ed's Perfect Tree

My older brother, Ed, was the artist in our family, and that included our annual Christmas tree. When it came to trimming the tree, we didn't throw tinsel on the branches. First the lights were carefully laid in place, then the colored balls hung in just the right places. I could help hang them, but only where Ed told me to put them. Then each length of tinsel was individually placed to the greatest advantage for beauty. Believe me, our tree was always the prettiest in town because of Ed's meticulous planning and management of the process.

One December, Ed went into the woods looking for a tree, which was not against the law then. Looking up, he saw the perfectly-shaped top of a moderately-sized tree. He climbed up and sawed off the top eight feet, built a platform for it, and brought it into the house. The tree was perfect in its symmetry, reaching all the way to the ceiling. That year Ed insisted on decorating the tree by himself. The result was a masterpiece of beauty.

Once again, visitors from the city came by on their way to visit Mount Rainier. They were stunned by the beauty of Ed's perfect Christmas tree. Then a miracle happened. The visitors had never seen such a perfectly symmetrical tree. They were so captivated by it that they made an astounding offer of $25 for the tree. At that time, $25 was an astronomical amount of money, more that Dad's cash income for several months.

Ed agreed to their offer. While the visitors went on up to the mountain, he removed all the decorations. After they returned, tied the tree onto their car, and drove away, Ed headed back into the woods. There he found another beautifully-shaped tree, but not quite as perfect as the first one. That year we had two Christmas trees and a life-saving infusion of money into our sparse family economy.

SIBLING REVELRY

We four young'uns were as normal as can be. We had our times of arguing, but fighting was not allowed. We were taught to love and respect one another, which we did for the most part. My oldest sister, Lilian, was born eleven years before I was. My mother's health was poor when I was preschool age, and Lilian took over as what I call "my other mother." Loving and caring, she watched over her baby brother like a mother. At age 94, she still calls me her "baby brother."

This was before the invention of today's technology. We had no television or computers and electronic games. But we did have family entertainment. We played a game called Caroms. Each person took twelve caroms (circles of wood with a large hole in the middle). Two sets were red and green. Each player used a white carom to shoot with. We did so on a board from behind a line by snapping the white carom. At the four corners were holes with nets below, something like a pool table. The first to get all of his or her caroms into the nets won.

We also enjoyed playing Rook. Two could play or any number. However, some of the people at church believed card playing was only for gamblers and that decent folks shouldn't play cards. So when we had a family game night, we pulled down the window shades so none of the card opponents could spy on us.

BEDTIME STORIES

Since I was the youngest child in the family, I was put to bed earlier than my siblings. I always asked for a bedtime story after I was tucked in. Either one of my parents or brother or a sister would do. They occasionally ran out of stories and repeated them from time to time. Ed was the most creative. He told me fascinating true stories he learned in school.

I hated it when they pulled "the girl with a curl" story on me. It lasted only a few seconds and left me upset while trying to go to sleep. The story went like this. "Once there was a little girl who had a curl in the middle of her forehead. When she was good, she was very good, but when she was bad she was horrid." Then, "Goodnight, Bobby," and a kiss on my forehead. I still hate the sound of that sorry story.

BUCKET BRIGADE
In National we didn't have an indoor bathroom. We used an outdoor "path to the bath," an outdoor toilet built over a deep hole in the ground. It featured two holes to sit on. I never figured out why there were two because we always used it one at a time.

At night, we didn't go out into the dark back yard where the toilet was located. Instead, we had a big bucket-like contraption with a lid. If anyone had to "go" during the night, we used what we called the "Slop Jar." In the morning, someone took the Slop Jar to the outdoor toilet and emptied it—a thankless job. Everyone hated marching in the bucket brigade.

PEE WEE
There's a funny story about my big brother, Ed. When he and Dad were building the parsonage, the two of them slept in the farmhouse across the road. There was no indoor bathroom in it either.

One night, Ed woke up "dying to pee." He went downstairs into the kitchen and tried to go out on the back porch. There he planned to pee out into the grass. But the door was locked and he couldn't get it open. The situation became critical. *He had to go!* With moonlight streaming in the kitchen window, Ed saw several glass tumblers sitting on the counter. He filled one, then another. With no place to empty them, he placed the glasses on the counter and went back upstairs to bed.

Early in the morning, the farmer and his wife got up and headed for the kitchen. The farmer said to his wife, "When did you make this jelly?" To their surprise, "this jelly" turned out to be two glasses of yellow urine. When everyone assembled for breakfast, the mystery was solved. Red-faced Ed admitted he was the culprit. He never heard the last of his making "jelly" during the night.

AFTER-SCHOOL SNACK

One of our favorite after-school events was when my brother and sisters walked home from school in nearby Ashford, possibly a half mile along the two-lane highway. Certain days became special when Mom baked homemade bread timed to come out of the oven just before they came in the door.

After washing our hands, we sat around the kitchen table with plates in front of us. Mom gave each of us a thick slab of warm bread fresh out of the oven. On that we put homemade butter. Over the butter we poured sweet canned blackberries. On top of that we slathered thick cream from on top of that morning's milk, over which we sprinkled sugar. Then with fork and spoon we dove in and ate the glorious combo of fabulous flavors. I've never eaten anything since then that could top that afternoon snack. In spite of that, we were hungry again for supper at six.

SIMPLE LIFESTYLE

We lived a simple but happy lifestyle. We were poor, but only Mom and Dad knew it. As I said earlier, even in the depths of the Great Depression we never missed a meal. We lived off the land, pound parties, and food relief tickets.

We always knew when Dad came home from the city with clothing from Good Will and maybe fresh doughnuts from the bakery and other things he brought for the family. Mom's favorite treat was candy-coated "burnt peanuts," and Dad usually brought a supply to her, which she shared with the family. Dad would turn off the engine of the Model T Ford and coast to a stop beside our house, hoping to surprise us. But the driveway of sorts was composed of gravel. When we heard the wheels in the gravel, we ran outside eager to see what Dad had brought home from the city. We were never disappointed.

TO BED WE GO

Some of us slept upstairs under the roof. I loved to fall asleep hearing rain pelting the roof over my head while I lay snug, warm, and dry under a quilt in my bed. I felt secure, protected, and loved. Who can ask for more than that?

Whenever one of us kids was sick, we got to sleep downstairs on the pullout "davenport." Mom pampered us with "cambric tea" to make us feel better. I learned later that "cambric tea" was made of hot water with milk and sugar in it. One time when I was "sick abed" with the flu, one of our rabbits gave birth to a litter. Dad brought a few of the cute little critters in and laid them on the quilt cover on my lap as I sat up. Their eyes weren't open yet, but they were soft to the touch and moved around looking for their mother. I enjoyed cuddling them until Dad took them back to their cage.

PICKING AT THE PIANO

We had an upright piano for our growing family. My two sisters took lessons from a teacher who came to our house. They were required to practice every day for their lessons.

With my inborn love of music and an ear for it, I could pick out the tunes I heard with one finger. My sisters learned the hard way, while I picked it up naturally, the way children learn to walk or talk. Playing piano came easily for me.

PAINFUL MEMORIES

As a preschool child I was afflicted with excruciating earaches. I woke up many nights crying from pain. Nothing anyone could do helped. My father took me to a doctor, but he found nothing he could fix. He suggested hospitalization, but it never went that far. Mom treated my earaches with warm oil, and I finally outgrew them.

DEALING WITH DEATH

The month I turned six, Grandpa Haslam died in Seattle. He, too, was a pastor all his adult life. I loved my grandpa dearly and he doted on me. I cried bitterly when he was gone.

We all piled into Dad's Model T Ford and headed toward Seattle for the funeral. The custom was an open casket at the wakes and funerals. Dad leaned over and kissed his father good-bye. He picked me up so I could see Grandpa one more time. Dad asked me if I wanted to touch Grandpa, but I said no, because I was afraid. This was the first time death became real to me. Grandpa's death was a terrible loss.

DRAMATIC DREAMS

For some reason, I experienced recurring identical dreams while we lived those four years in National. Three of them stand out in my memory; I can still visualize them decades later.

BUTLER'S BULL

Down the road a ways was the Butler farm where Mr. Butler owned a mean bull. Occasionally, Butler's bull broke through the fence and the men in town turned out to corral him. His ferocious twists and turns bamfoozled the men, but eventually they got him back in his field. They immediately repaired the fence to keep him in.

In my dream, all four of us kids were playing beside the house. Butler's bull came charging into our yard and the older three ran into the house, but my legs wouldn't move. The bull knocked me to the ground and began eating me feet first. My dream ended with my being eaten up to my waist. I waved good-bye to my brother and sisters as they waved good-bye to me through the safety of the window as the bull gobbled me down. I awoke in a sweat and went crying to my parents' bedroom. They calmed me down and took me back to my bed and tucked me in.

EATEN BY A WOLF

Another dream was also dramatic and fearful. One of the stories told me by my siblings was about a little boy who was eaten by a wolf. In my dream there was a pound party at night and the children went out into the darkness to play. I dreamed that when I wandered away from the others, a wolf came out of the woods and ate me. One child saw what happened and went inside yelling, *"Bobby's been eaten by a wolf!"* I saw and heard that from inside my captor. Each time I dreamed it I woke up crying for help.

DIVINE DREAM

I recall one beautiful recurring dream that topped them all. It was suggested into my subconscious mind by sermons my father preached about heaven and Jesus' words that some day he will return to Earth. Dad also talked about God's storehouse of blessings. These all came out in the following ways.

In my dream, I went out after dark onto our back porch. There in the yard stood my father talking to Jesus, who looked like the pictures I had seen in Sunday school papers. When Jesus gestured toward the sky, I looked up and saw large shelves filled with all kinds of food. This represented the storehouse of heaven's blessings I had heard about. Still in my dream, I turned and ran back into the house yelling at the top of my voice to wake up the rest of the family to come see Jesus with Dad in our back yard. At this point my dream ended. After this dream, I laid in bed with a warm fuzzy feeling that all was well with my world.

TRAFFIC TANTALIZER

One time as I played in front of our house with a friend, cars passed travelling both ways on the highway. I don't remember whose idea it was, but we went out into the middle of the highway and stood there as cars approached daring them to hit us, then, at the last second ran to the side of the road. One driver applied the brakes and came to a screeching stop. My friend and I climbed over the gate of the farm across the road and hurrried into the wheat field that had been harvested. We ran a ways and crouched behind a mound of hay and stayed hidden. The driver came looking for us, but couldn't find us. I think he was so mad he wanted to "whup" us good.

He went to the parsonage and asked my mother if she had two little boys. She admitted to having one who was playing with another. When the angry driver told my mother what we had done, she called for me to come. While my friend remained safely hidden behind a hay mound, I sheepishly came out of hiding, crossed the highway, and faced the angry man and my concerned mother. The rest of the story wasn't pretty. I never did that again.

STICKY FINGERS

My sister, Irene, and I walked a few doors away so she could visit her girlfriend, June. While they were playing, I hung around and amused myself. I came across a toy I thought I'd like to take home with me and hid it in my clothing. I decided to go home ahead of my sister. When I came to the church, I saw a perfect place to hide the toy. I knew I couldn't take it in the house, because Mom would ask where I got it. The country church was built up on blocks of wood with a crawl space under it. I hid the toy under the church behind a block of wood.

The next day I remembered the toy and asked my mother if I could go outside to play. She said yes, but when I went to retrieve the toy, to my horror it was gone. Fear and panic seized me. Someone must have seen me take the toy and hide it. But who? The uncertainty drove me nuts. I ran back into our house to play. Mom wanted to know why, and I gave her a lame excuse. I was fearful my sticky-fingered episode would come back to haunt me, but it never did.

SOAPY SUDS

My brother Ed played the guitar and we sang silly songs that were popular. One was about a man who did something wrong and ended up in the calaboose (jail). Once when we were singing it I pronounced calaboose as "hell-aboose." Father forbade our using any swear words or even slang words.

One of my siblings told Dad that I had sung "hell-aboose." He marched me into the kitchen, picked up a bar of Ivory soap, and rubbed it into my teeth to cleanse my mouth from evil speaking. After all, they advertised that Ivory soap was 99 and 44/100 percent pure. I gagged and spit. It was hours before the taste of soap left my mouth. Small wonder, then, that in my growing up years, and to this day, my language has been "clean." A little soap goes a long way toward bringing about that result.

TURNS IN THE TUB

You may have wondered about baths at our household in National since we had an outdoor toilet. Saturday night was bath night at our house. Mother heated water on the wood stove and poured it into a large round tub on the floor. If it was too hot, Mom added cold water. If it got cool, she poured in more hot water.

We took turns going into the kitchen, taking off our clothes, sitting in the tub, using the same water, soaping up, rinsing off, then drying with a towel. That way we were all spic-and-span clean for church on Sunday morning. Many years later, when my family and I were in the Philippines, we used a similar method when water became scarce during dry seasons.

WANDERING IN THE WOODS

I loved to roam through the woods back of our house. Mother let me go by myself to wander among the trees and admire the wild flowers. It was safe back then. If it was late morning, Mom told me to hurry back to the house when the noon lumber mill whistle blew. The loud piercing sound could be heard for miles. It meant it was time for the workers to eat their lunch. Those who lived nearby went home to eat.

When I was in the woods my favorite places were clearings surrounded by trees that were like outdoor rooms. I laid down on the ground on my back and looked up into the towering trees above. I walked through the woods, breathed lots of fresh air, and fell in love with nature. It was better than sitting in front of a TV or playing fingertip gadget games, which we didn't have then.

HOMEMADE REFRIGERATION

We didn't have a refrigerator in National to keep milk and food fresh, but we managed to do it in two ways. The first method was a built-in cooler. When Dad built the house, in the kitchen's back outside wall he cut a hole in the outer wall, placed a screen across it, and built a cabinet with doors on the inside. The screen kept out the varmints and let in fresh air. During winter months it kept everything in it cool. In summer it became storage for non-perishable items.

Best of all was a large cabinet with a door called an icebox. It had a space to place a fairly large block of ice. This was surrounded by shelves for milk and other food that would deteriorate in warm air. Every few days Dad went to the icehouse and brought home a new block of ice. That was our "refrigerator."

GOOSEBERRY PIE

I've mentioned our picking wild berries in the woods and logged-off hillsides. For the most part, they were large, juicy, and delicious. These included lush blackberries, "black caps" (black raspberries), red raspberries, huckleberries, salmon berries, and even wild strawberries. And then there were the gooseberries, round yellowish-green berries that were very sour. However, a generous amount of sugar could make them tolerable.

My sister, Irene, and her best friend, June, decided to pick gooseberries and make a pie. They made a solemn vow to each other that no matter what the outcome, they would eat the pie. One problem—they forgot to include sugar in the ingredients. This gave rise to extremely sour results. They begged me, little brother, to eat a generous portion of the pie, but I declined. Did the girls honor their pledge and eat all the sour pie? They will carry that secret to their graves.

GRAPE JUICE BOMB

My brother, Ed, learned at school that wine was made with grape juice and yeast, which is also used in bread to make it rise. Mom always had yeast on hand for making bread. When Ed found grape juice in the pantry, he took a bottle with a screw-top lid and "borrowed" grape juice and a smidgen of yeast. He mixed them together, screwed the cap on tightly, and took the bottle to the attic to see if he could make wine.

Time passed and Ed forgot about his experiment. Meanwhile, the heat in the attic was intense during the day, which helped the fermentation to proceed. A loud explosion took place in the attic. We all heard it and rushed upstairs to see what happened. In the attic, broken glass and fermented grape juice were all over the place, and it stunk to high heaven. When Dad asked who created the mess, Ed finally confessed. His punishment was to clean up the mess.

SPIRITUAL AWAKENING

My earliest recollections of my childhood in National are of our "family altar." Each day we gathered and placed six chairs in a circle for Mom, Dad, and four kids. First we sang a hymn or gospel song from memory, then someone read from the Bible. After sharing prayer requests, we went around the circle and each person prayed. That's how I learned to pray. At first, someone said a few words of prayer and I repeated them. Then a few more words for me to repeat. After a time I began to pray my own simple, short prayers. It was a natural way to learn.

Since Dad was a pastor, our family attended church almost every time a service was held. I loved Sunday school where the teachers told us Bible stories about people who loved and honored God. Each Sunday, the teachers gave each of us a take-home paper with stories and pictures in it. I persuaded one of my family members to read it to me Sunday afternoon—after my nap. My spiritual awareness was beautifully developed by my own family and my church family. The love and spiritual nurture I received are things I am deeply grateful for.

One Sunday two women came to our church in National from the American Sunday School Union. They traveled to rural churches to share Bible stories with children and used pictures painted on flannel cloth that stuck to a felt background on a board standing on an easel/tripod. I had never seen such bright pictures in story form before. One lady put up the pictures while the other told the story.

The first background was blue sky above and green grass below. Then the lady put up a brown hill. On the hillside she placed three crosses, and on them she put the figures of three men. The lady telling the story talked about Jesus, who was on the center cross with a criminal on each side of him. She explained that Jesus did not deserve the punishment of dying on a cross, but did it so he could pay the penalty for our sins. As a preschool child with my family and church background, I understood what she was saying.

Then she spoke of how much God loved us to send his Son to die for our sins. She said that if we would open our hearts, Jesus would come in and be our Savior. That Sunday morning I opened my heart to Jesus. He has been there ever since.

CHAPTER THREE
Starting School; My First Cigarette

Bobby, Lilian, Irene and Ed in Olympia

*"If we confess our sins, he is faithful and just
and will forgive us our sins...."
(1 John 1:9)*

CULTURE SHOCK

T he summer I was six, we moved to Olympia, the capital city of the state of Washington. Dad was the new pastor there, and that fall I entered first grade. Culture shock takes place when moving from a tiny town to a bustling big city, at least when you've just turned six.

The contrast was almost total. From plank roads to paved streets. From substandard housing with outhouses to modern homes with indoor plumbing. From a quiet country atmosphere to a city where anything and everything happens. From tall trees to tall buildings. From bare survival living to a more comfortable economy. From a town without a traffic light to a city filled with them.

It took some adjusting for a boy who loved to wander in the woods, only to land in a concrete jungle. Some of the changes were good. I missed other things back in National.

Instead of a cow with plenty of milk, cream, and homemade butter, our milk was delivered by a milkman early in the morning from a dairy on the edge of town. Milk wasn't homogenized, so the quart bottle, with a cardboard cap on top, was quite a change.

We moved all of Mom's canned food to Olympia. The vegetables and meat were fine, but the berries lost their attractiveness because we lacked the thick cream and home-churned butter we were accustomed to. Mom donated dozens of jars of berries to a charity. No more after-school bread with the fabulous fixin's. It took time, yet after a while I felt at home in Olympia, but life was entirely different.

STARTING SCHOOL

A few weeks after we moved, I entered first grade at Washington Elementary School. We lived within walking distance, and now there were four of us in school. Irene and I attended Washington, while Ed and Lilian were in high school across town.

The first day of first grade, the principal came into our room to welcome us. He told us we had a lot to learn. He asked if anyone knew the result of multiplying 12 x 12. It was a dumb question to ask first graders on their first day. And I was dumb enough to try and answer it. I had an advantage. My older siblings practiced their multiplication tables out loud at home, so I had heard that 12 x 12 = 144. So when the principal asked the question, I raised my hand.

"What's the answer, young man?"

"Four hundred and forty-four," I replied.

For shame! I took my earliest opportunity to prove how smart I was and gave a wrong answer.

SISSY STUFF

When I started school during warm fall days, my mother dressed me in short pants, but I quickly saw that all the other boys wore long pants. I told Mom, but she didn't take me seriously. She still laid out short pants for me to wear to school.

At recess, a group of older boys, I guess in third or fourth grade, formed a circle around me and pointed at me while chanting, "Sissy wears bloomers! Sissy wears bloomers!" I was humiliated, and went home and told Mom what happened. From that day on, she laid out long pants for me to wear.

THE SITUATION GOT BLADDER

Never having sat in school for hours at a time, I was in the habit of going to the bathroom whenever I needed to. Soon after day one, I was "dying to pee." I raised my hand and the teacher motioned for me to come to her desk. I asked permission to go to the restroom.

"Wait until recess," she replied.

I returned to my seat, but couldn't wait. Soon there was a puddle under my seat. Someone told the teacher, and only then did she tell me I could go to the restroom, but it was too late. When I went home and told my folks, they contacted my teacher and told her about my problem. She took me aside and quietly told me I could go to the restroom anytime without asking.

HIGH DRAMA

Our teacher decided that we first graders would put on a play in our classroom. I've never been good at memorizing, so I didn't volunteer. But that didn't matter. My teacher, Miss Hoppy, "volunteered" my services.

Acting the part of a little bird, I tried to memorize two short sentences. "To wit, to wit, to wee. Will you listen to me?" The day of our production arrived, and I was in place. Each kid in turn spoke their lines. Then it was my turn, and my mind went blank.

Miss Hoppy whispered, "To wit...."

I froze.

"To wit, to wit..."

Aha. Then I remembered it. Embarrassed and ashamed, I hoarsely whispered what I was supposed to shout: "To wit, to wit, to wee. Will you listen to me?" I never again got involved in drama productions, because I was afraid I'd forget my lines.

MEASELY MOMENTS

When I was a kid, we didn't have vaccinations for childhood diseases. One of my classmates contracted "infantile paralysis," which is now called polio.

When it came to the measles, I was infected twice. The first was German measles, also called the three-day measles, which was no big deal. Later I contracted a more serious strain known as Red Measles, or the two-week measles. "When the doctor diagnosed my case, he informed the health department. That day a health department official came and posted a "quarantine" sign by our front door. For two weeks no one but family members could enter. This was bad news for my father whose office was in the parsonage rather than the church. People often came to see him. But now, our house was off limits.

The doctor said that because of that kind of measles, I must stay in a dark room for two weeks with the window shades pulled all the way down to protect my eyes, otherwise my eyes would be damaged. Even though we complied with his order, I developed "weak eyes" from the ordeal. To this day I have good vision, but my eyes are sensitive to bright light.

PLAYING WITH POLLYWOGS

My all-time favorite grade in school was third. My teacher, Mrs. Norris, made learning fun. One time we had a project about cave men. We brought in cardboard boxes that we flattened and created a big brown cave we could take turns crawling into.

Mrs. Norris brought to class a fairly-good-sized fish tank and asked if any of us could bring in frogs' eggs. I raised my hand, because on my way to school there was an empty lot with a stagnant pool, and I heard frogs croaking. She told me what to look for.

That afternoon after school I went home and got an empty glass jar with a lid. I took it to the pond and found along the edge a batch of tiny gray round eggs that looked like tapioca pudding. I scooped them into the jar and took them to school the next day. Mrs. Norris had me empty the jar into the fish tank that held water.

We watched every day until a black spot appeared in each egg. Later the spots grew and began to move and eventually wormed their way out of the eggs. They moved around by swishing their tails. We kept watching until little legs appeared on the bodies of the pollywogs. Eventually the tails fell off and the pollywogs were now little frogs.

Fourth grade wasn't nearly as much fun as third.

A HOLE IN THE HEAD

Christmas was approaching, our tree was decorated, and Mom had filled a bowl with hard candy. She noticed that I was into the candy too often, so she put it up on a high protruding shelf of our China cabinet. On a Wednesday night, Mom and Dad went next door to church, and I was left at home to go to bed early because of school. My older sister, Lilian, stayed home to supervise me.

I was in my pajamas and eyed that candy up too high for me to reach. I stood up on the seat of a rocking chair, but still couldn't reach the candy. Then I did something stupid and dangerous. I stood on the arm of the rocking chair and leaned out reaching for the candy. When the rocking chair began to rock, I lost my balance and jumped down to the floor. I was falling so ran with my head down trying to get my balance.

Wham! My head collided with a sharp corner of the piano bench. It penetrated my head between my eyes causing a deep hole in my forehead. It began bleeding profusely. Lilian ran to the church and interrupted the prayer meeting to get Dad. He hurried home, took me to the bathroom, and tried to clean up my wound. It was hopeless, continuing to bleed.

Lilian held a towel against my forehead while Dad called the doctor. He agreed to meet us at his office. When we arrived, the doctor uttered the dreaded words, "It looks like I'm going to have to sew up this wound." After putting in the stitches, the doctor placed a bandage on my forehead. All for a piece of candy I was not supposed to have in the first place—and didn't get! I still have a nice scar to prove my story.

FOOLISH FINGER FIASCO

One summer day Dad was cutting tall grass along the side of the street. While holding a clump of grass in his left hand, he cut it off at the ground level with a sickle. I wanted to try my hand at doing it, but the phone rang and Mom called Dad into the house. Dad told me not to use the sickle until he returned.

When Dad disappeared into the house, I picked up the sickle with my right hand, held a clump of grass with my left hand, and—*ouch!* I hit the end of my left index finger with the edge of the sickle causing a deep gash. I ran screaming into the house. Dad excused himself from his phone conversation and tended to my wound. I carried that scar for many years.

FALLING OFF A LADDER

A large cherry tree towered behind our neighbors' house. These were orange and yellow orbs then called Royal Anne cherries, now renamed Rainier cherries. A ladder was leaning into the tree, and an adult had picked the easy-to-reach cherries. I asked permission to climb the ladder. With their consent, I climbed up and was about to enjoy an afternoon snack. Since someone had already picked the area clean, I went to the left side of the ladder and leaned way out trying to reach a cluster of delicious Royal Annes.

The ladder began to slide, and both the ladder and I headed for the ground. I jumped off and landed flat on my back, knocking the air out of my lungs. As I gasped for breath, I noticed half of my body didn't work. My entire left side went numb. With difficulty I crawled all the way home, up the steps, and told my folks what happened. They were greatly concerned.

My mother was being treated by a chiropractor at that time, so Dad called him. Could he treat me immediately? Dad told him my back was injured. Sure enough, when the chiropractor ran his fingers up and down my spine, some of my vertebrae were out of position. He first used damp heat and liniment, then straightened my crooked back, at least for that time.

Later, when I was in college and had a complete physical exam, an X-ray determined that there was a pyramid effect in my spine. Two vertebrae were partly behind a middle one, creating a lump. Technicians put a body cast on my back and chest while I leaned forward. When I straightened up, the cast pulled the vertebrae into line. I wore the plaster cast for six weeks. All for a Royal Anne cherry I never got to eat.

COFFEE CAPER

After Grandpa Haslam died, Grandma sometimes came to stay with us for a week or two. She told my father to always keep Hills Brothers Coffee on hand, as she must have Hills Brothers brewed every morning. She insisted she could tell the difference between that and any other brand of coffee.

Over time, Grandma used up the large can of coffee in her visits. When she was scheduled to come the next time, Dad bought the cheapest coffee he could find and poured those coffee grounds into the empty Hills Brothers can. When Grandma came, she went to the cupboard and found the can. She made her coffee and bragged that it was the best in town. No one ever told her the difference.

PRIEST IN THE PARSONAGE

In those days, we had revival meetings at church in the fall and again in the spring. Dad scheduled evangelists to speak in the nightly services. On the recommendation of another pastor, he scheduled Rev. Walter S. Kendall to be our next speaker. What Dad did not know was that Rev. Kendall wore a clerical collar. A knock came at the front door,

Mother opened it, and there stood a man with a suitcase wearing a clerical collar. Mom thought he was a Catholic priest and told him he had come to the wrong church. Rev. Kendall laughed and introduced himself as our scheduled speaker. Mom never lived that down.

Rev. Kendall doted on me and called me Bobby. Many years later when he became a bishop, I worked at the church headquarters in the missions office. The first time Bishop Kendall saw me, he said, "Welcome to Winona Lake, Bobby!" Then he added, "OOPS! I shouldn't call you that now that you're a grown man." From then on he addressed me as "Brother Haslam."

SPELLING BEE

Uncle Ed, Aunt Ella and Cousin Isabelle came for a visit. Isabelle was about my sister Irene's age. My parents and aunt and uncle sat in the living room while Irene, Isabelle and I were in the kitchen where Irene was making fudge for our guests.

Somewhere in our kitchen conversation the subject of using bad language came up. Our family was forbidden to speak that way. I mentioned to the girls that during recess that day one of the boys had used a naughty word. Irene and Isabelle pressed me to tell them the word, but I was afraid to. I wasn't interested in any more soap in my mouth.

They offered a compromise. "Spell it," Irene said. It took some persuading, but finally I agreed to her proposal. Irene said to whisper the letters, and we got close to one another so they could hear me. However, we were in such a silly mood that when I spelled sh--, I was laughing out loud so it came out as a shout rather than a whisper.

Unhappily for me, just then a pause occurred in the conversation in the living room and my parents, aunt and uncle heard me laughingly spell a naughty word. My father was not one to postpone action when one of his kids got out of line.

Suddenly father appeared in the kitchen. Without saying a word, he took me by the arm and marched me not to the bathroom to put soap in my teeth. No, my punishment was to be led into the living room and seated with the adults. No one spoke for a while. I sat there mortified and embarrassed, then conversation resumed. There I sat, guilty as can be, shamed by being with those who disapproved of what I had done. I would have preferred the soap.

This spelling bee turned out to have a stinger in it.

FINGER IN THE FUDGE

Speaking of fudge, my sister, Irene, was the family fudge maker. She boiled the contents on the stove, beat it by hand, and poured it into a greased pan to cool and harden. Irene hated to put her hands in lard to grease the pan. She and I made an agreement that when she made fudge, I greased the pan in exchange for my being permitted to take a spoon and scrape and eat what remained of the fudge in the boiler after she poured it into the greased pan. She always left a little extra in appreciation for my getting my hands greasy instead of hers.

One time in Olympia, when I was around eight years old, the fudge was boiling away on the stove and I couldn't wait to taste it. I tried to swipe my finger across the top of the boiling candy and get just enough on my finger to taste it. I made a couple of test swipes when suddenly Irene slapped my hand and forced my entire finger down into the boiling goo.

I screamed at the top my lungs and ran to the sink to wash the hot fudge off with cold water. Cold water hardened it and my finger was ablaze with pain. Mother rushed into the kitchen to see what all the yelling was about. I told on my sister and Mother pronounced the consequences. First, she told me I shouldn't have done what I was trying to do, but for Irene, there was an outcome. She was to finish making the fudge, but when it cooled and hardened she was forbidden to eat any of it.

Well, guess what—*she fudged!*

THE BIG BLIZZARD

Our church and parsonage were up on a hill on the east side of Olympia. From our corner at 1425 Legion Way, the street sloped steeply downhill. There was a double or triple block without side streets before Legion Way bottomed out and became level again alongside Washington Elementary School.

One year, an unusual event occurred—a blizzard—not what you would expect in the state of Washington along the coast of the warm waters of the Puget Sound. Because our street was so steep, the street department put up barriers at the intersection because cars could not safely travel either up or down the slippery slope.

People came from all over the city to ride down the slope on sleds, toboggans, and even on skis. Our church's wood furnace heated the building, so there was a winter's supply of wood stacked behind the building. Enterprising celebrants "borrowed" wood from behind the church and made a huge bonfire to warm themselves between trips down the slope. It was a festive time as crowds of people came to enjoy the winter wonderland in front of our house.

EXPLOSIVE LEARNING

Fast-forward from winter on our hillside to the Fourth of July. Olympia is in a valley with hills to the east and west. From our windows or yard we watched as people across town on the western slopes set off fireworks.

My father, who was an expert with math and science, knew lots of things he taught us kids. One was on a Fourth of July. Dad's watch ticked off seconds, as well as minutes and hours. When we saw a bright explosion across town on the western slopes, Dad counted the seconds until we heard the boom. Folks over there set off powerful fireworks. Dad taught us that the speed of sound is 1,125 feet per second, or 768 miles per hour. He computed the number of seconds to determine how far away the fireworks explosions were. This was one of my first lessons in "higher math."

CAPITAL COLLECTION

Dad was an avid stamp collector. He collected both used and mint (unused) stamps. My brother Ed and I picked up the hobby from Dad and did our best to fill stamp books with all the U.S. stamps that were printed, as well as those from foreign countries.

I don't know how he found out, but Dad discovered that in the basement of the state capitol building were large trash bins filled with material from the wastebaskets of the offices. Frequently, we went to the capitol building, sorted through the trash bins, and took envelopes that had commemorative stamps on them. We often came away with hundreds of them. Most were U.S. stamps, but some were from foreign countries. It was like a treasure chest for collectors.

One time Dad found an envelope that was still sealed with an interesting stamp on it. The next day, he took it to the office of the official named on the envelope. When the official opened it, he found a sizeable check. He thanked Dad for bringing it to him and said he was glad we were searching in the trash bins. In appreciation, he gave Dad the envelope with the pretty stamp.

I collected new and used stamps for decades. Later in life it all paid off. When we were about to build a new house, I sold my collection of mint plate number blocks that went back many years. That netted almost a thousand dollars to help cover the down payment on our house in Warsaw, Indiana. Later, when we lived in Michigan, I saw a group of stamp dealers' kiosks in a mall. I talked with one dealer who agreed to come to our house and look through my collection of thousands of used and mint stamps. One commemorative sheet of United Nations stamps with a face value of less than one dollar brought me a nice return of $50. The total he paid for my remaining stamps was hundreds of dollars, which I invested in my first computer.

It all began when I was in the second grade in Olympia, diving into trash bins looking for colorful commemorative stamps.

CLAMMING UP

The city of Olympia is located at the southern end of the Puget Sound, a large protected body of water that is an extension of the Pacific Ocean. Thus, it is made up of salt water. It was okay for swimming, but swimmers always experience the taste of salt.

On occasion, our church family held an outing at the beach during low tide so we could dig for clams. I always took a small shovel and bucket and filled it to the brim. With everyone digging, we always came back to the parsonage with good results. My mother put big boilers on the woodburning stove and heated the water to the boiling point. When the clams went into the water, they cooked up for a delicious feast. We all had our fill on those occasions.

MY FIRST PAYING JOB

On one occasion I was playing in the front yard when a car drove up and stopped in front of our house. A man in the car opened the window and called me over. Today, kids are taught to run the other way, but this turned out okay.

"Would you like to make some money?" the man asked.

"Sure."

"You can make money by going to your neighbors and taking orders for the *Saturday Evening Post*. Would you like to do that?"

I told him I would.

He gave me a sample copy and explained that when I collected for the magazine, I could keep a nickel for each one. *A nickel!* In my seven-year-old Depression economy, that was a lot. I told my folks and they directed me to nearby streets where I could safely knock on doors. It worked. I became a capitalist with my first taste of regular income from my very own sales and delivery business.

A GAY TIME

In my early grades, Dad knew I would hear older boys talking about sex on the school grounds, so he clued me in. At various times we "had a talk" about the human anatomy and where babies come from. So early in life, I was "in the know."

But my dad never mentioned homosexuality, as it was called then. I was totally unaware that it existed, until one Sunday my folks let me go home for dinner with a farm family that included young boys. After dinner, the oldest boy escorted us to the barn where we climbed a ladder to the loft. Up there, this older boy said that if I would let him put his xxx in my xxx, then he would let me put my xxx in his xxx. I was horrified at the thought and was terribly afraid of what he might do to me.

I said no, and he persisted a while, then gave up. We went down from the loft and I could hardly wait until we drove back for the evening church service and the safety of home. The next time we "had a talk," I told Dad about my experience. I never went home with that farm family again, possibly because my father spoke with the boy's parents.

CAPITAL CRIME SPREE

CRIME # 1
Living in the capital city, I got into things I would have never gotten into back in National. I was in Olympia during grades one through three.

Mom asked me to go to the Hillcrest Market, one block from our house, to get cooking supplies. When I walked into the small store, the owner was in the back room and hadn't heard me come in. As I stood there, I noticed packages of nickel gum that looked inviting. They weren't on Mom's list, but on an impulse I can't explain, I reached up, took a package of gum, and put it in my pocket. Soon after, the owner came out. "Hi, Bobby! What can I do for you today?" I gave him the list, paid with Mom's money, and went home.

Years later, driving through Olympia I went out of my way to confess my sin and pay $5.00 (including interest) for stealing the gum. Sadly, the Hillcrest Market had been torn down to build a bank on that corner. The Good Lord knows I tried to make restitution for my capital crime.

CRIME #2

In my family smoking was a no-no, but I found a way around that rule. I was with some boys in a wheat field where an ornery weed called "Indian tobacco" also grew. It has a stalk with small branches that are surrounded by clusters of small brown buds. When they are dry, you can strip the buds off of the plant and hold in your hand "Indian tobacco."

At the edge of the field was a spreading chestnut tree. The oldest kid picked up a large nut and with his pocket knife dug out the interior, leaving a neat brown bowl with an open top. He then, with the point of his knife, bored a small hole in one side of the chestnut. He picked a large wheat straw, cut it down to size, and inserted it into the hole. Next he stripped Indian tobacco off a plant and put it in the chestnut. He created a home-made pipe. He had matches with him and we all took turns smoking the "peace pipe." That was my introduction to the crime (in my family) of smoking.

CRIME #3

The fun of smoking Indian tobacco wasn't forgotten. On the corner in front of our church was a bus stop. Often, people who were smoking threw down their cigarettes before getting on the bus. I noticed that some of the cigarette stubs were tantalizingly long enough to smoke again. When I was in first grade, I began picking them up and taking them behind the church where wood for the church furnace was stacked. A space was left between the back of the church and the ends of the sawed wood. I put my back against the church and walked up by stepping on yet higher pieces of wood. I hid the cigarettes up above.

I "borrowed" matches from the kitchen, went to my "loft," and smoked the stubs. Then I went home and brushed my teeth to eliminate the tobacco smell. This was before cigarette filters were invented, so I inhaled a high level of nicotine. I don't know how long this went on, but it's a miracle no one ever caught me smoking or smelled tobacco on me. Finally I decided to quit pushing my luck, and without the use of aids to stop smoking, I quit my "addiction" to tobacco cold turkey.

Now, when a health professional asks me if I've ever smoked, I reply that I quit smoking when I was six years old.

It was well into my adult years before I ever confessed to my parents that I had smoked cigarette butts behind the old wooden church in Olympia. Dad's only reply was, "It's a wonder you didn't burn the church down."

CRIME #4

This one is serious. It could have been tragic.

One hot summer afternoon, my sister Lilian and I were the only ones home. Since she's eleven years older than I am, she was in charge. I asked permission to go outside and play, and she agreed.

Across the side street was a corner lot on a small rise covered with summer-dried Scotch Bloom. On both sides of that corner lot were homes. I went across the street and saw that even the grass was dried and brown along the sidewalk. I went home and took a few matches from the kitchen.

I returned and had fun starting little grass fires and stomping them out. It was fun until the fire ran up the side of the rise toward the very dry Scotch Bloom. I tried in vain to stop it. As fast as my legs could carry me, I ran home and shouted for Lilian to call the fire department. I ran to our back yard and watched as flames from the scotch bloom leaped higher and higher. Quickly, a fire truck arrived and in no time the fire was out. Again, not for many years did I tell my parents about that escapade.

Alas, such was not the case on the part of one of our neighbors. After the fire, the next time I delivered the *Saturday Evening Post* across the street from the front of the church, the lady invited me in. "Sit down," she said rather sternly.

"I saw you playing with matches and I know you started the fire across the corner. I know you didn't mean to do it, but it happened. The fire could have destroyed many homes. I've been thinking of telling your father, and if I ever see you playing with matches again, I'll call him."

That was the end of my capital crime spree.

A FOND MEMORY OF OLYMPIA

During the three years we lived in Olympia, something occurred several times that remains etched in my memory. On Sunday mornings following the church service, Mr. or Mrs. Gibson occasionally said to me, "Bobby, would you like to go home with us for the afternoon? We'll bring you back to church this evening."

I don't recall ever not being allowed to go home with them. The Gibsons owned and managed a good-sized farm out in Lacy, a suburban farming area. Today Lacy is built up with subdivisions where the farms used to be, but then it was a locality featuring prosperous farms.

When we arrived, Mrs. Gibson prepared a scrumptious meal of meat, veggies, and always a wonderful pie for dessert. I ate until I couldn't hold another bite. Then I went out and wandered over the farm accompanied by Lady, a beautiful golden collie. We walked over fields, through trees, saw cows, horses, pigs, chickens...you name it, whatever is found on a large farm. Lady and I came to be great friends. We never had a dog in our home, so I loved spending time with her.

When I tired of that, I went back in the house. Like any grandmother, Mrs. Gibson said, Bobby, you've been out in the sun, now you need to rest. Lie down here on the sofa. Their sofa was soft and cushy. Sometimes I dozed off with the warm feeling of being pampered. After supper we got in the car or truck and drove back to church, where I rejoined my family.

Later, when the television program about Lassie was being aired, Lassie reminded me of Lady. They could have been twins.

CHAPTER FOUR
Lead Me Not Into Temptation

—◆—

At Burlington Campground: Lilian, Irene, Bob, Dad, Mom

Bob after shedding his bangs

Bob (sitting) with Ed, Irene, Lilian and Keith

Bob with a cute friend

*"No temptation has seized you except
what is common to man.
And God is faithful; he will not let you be tempted
beyond what you can bear.
But when you are tempted,
he will also provide you a way out
so that you can stand up under it."*
(1 Corinthians 10:13)

ANOTHER BIG CHANGE

A fter three years in Olympia, the bishop appointed my father to pastor the church in Burlington, Washington. The truck was loaded with all our earthly belongings, and we got in our car and headed north. We drove sixty miles from Olympia to Seattle, passing through Tacoma. After going through Everett, we hit the open road on U.S. Highway 99 and drove through rural areas to Burlington, around 70 miles north of Seattle, a total of about 130 miles.

As we drove into Burlington, we read the sign: Burlington: Population 1,407. This was a big change from the bustling city of Olympia. Nestled in the Skagit Valley, Burlington was where many dairy and produce farmers shopped and brought products to the grocery stores and meat markets. On any given day, especially Saturday, people came from the surrounding area to shop. But when we went to bed, there were only 1,407 of us.

I took an immediate liking to my new home town. Our house was located one long block from the high school where my brother Ed attended. My sister, Irene, and I walked the many blocks through town to Lincoln Grade School. Conveniently, the city library was across the street from school. The town people were friendly, our church family accepted us warmly, and we soon felt at home. This transition was much easier for me than moving from tiny National to the big city life of Olympia.

CLASS CLOWN

Beginning school in a new town is a drag. After three years in Washington School in Olympia, I knew just about everybody, especially in my grade. But now I was "the new boy on the block." Most of the kids knew each other, but I didn't know anyone. This is one of the hazards of being a preacher's kid, especially in the days when pastors were moved from one church to another every three or four years. Gradually, I got to know several kids pretty well. We went out together at recesses, and on the school grounds I became acquainted with other kids.

My teacher, whom I liked a lot, was Miss Blade. I had liked all my teachers up to that time and was relieved to have another good one. She kept the class under control, but was a person of good humor and laughed with us when someone said something funny.

One kid in our class was very much a clown. He brought laughter to our class frequently. Miss Blade wrote spelling words on the blackboard for us to copy, and proceeded to say each word correctly so we would know the proper pronunciation. Jimmy, the clown, played dumb when she said "pupil."

"What?" he asked.

"Pupil."

"What?"

"Pupil."

"What?"

"PEW-PILL!" Miss Blade shouted. The class exploded with laughter as Miss Blade laughed with us while her face turned red. Jimmy had worked his magic again.

A PLEASANT SURPRISE

Miss Blade welcomed a visitor to our room. When she walked in, I could hardly believe my eyes. It was Mrs.

Norris who had been my teacher the previous year in Olympia.

The class was assigned work to do at our desks, but I couldn't take my eyes off Mrs. Norris. Timid as I was, I got up and walked over to where the two ladies were talking in low tones.

"What is it, Bobby?" asked Miss Blade.

Mrs. Norris looked at me and squealed with delight. Just as everyone in the class looked up to see what was happening, Mrs. Norris leaned over and gave me a hug. That's when *my* face turned red.

AN UNEXPECTED SURPRISE

When I was in school, only single women were allowed to teach. Virtually every teacher was Miss whatever. Mrs. Norris was a widow with a son a grade ahead of me, so she was given a contract. One day, Miss Blade came to school wearing an engagement ring. None of us boys noticed, but the girls did. We supposed she would teach the rest of the year, and then get married.

Toward the middle of the first semester, Miss Blade made a stunning announcement. She told us that at the end of the month, she was leaving to get married. She added that this meant we would have a new teacher. The girls cried, and the boys groaned. Someone called out, "Can't you wait until the end of the year?"

"No, I'm getting married next month."

I don't remember the name of the teacher who took her place, partly because I remember nothing about her. Miss Blade was one of my favorite teachers, but her replacement was not.

FALSE FEVER

One warm spring day while in fourth grade, I was sweating out the heat like everyone else with no air conditioning. As the afternoon dragged on, I felt awful. I felt my forehead and it was hot. I went to the teacher and told her I thought I might have a temperature. She sent me to the principal's office next to our room. The school secretary put a thermometer under my tongue. Just then the principal, Mr. Cleveland, came out of his office and told his secretary to take a note around to the teachers announcing a baseball game between our school and another one across the street in the park after school.

Hearing that, no way did I want to go home early. I sucked air under my tongue so the thermometer would not show if I had a temperature. When the secretary took out the thermometer, it showed that my temperature was below normal. *Great!* I thought.

"Mr. Cleveland, Bobby's temperature is below normal. Is he okay to stay in school?"

"No, I think you should send him home."

"I'm feeling better now," I piped up.

Mr. Cleveland came out of his room, winked at the secretary, and said, "We don't want to take any chances, Bobby. You go on home." *Rats! Double rats! Triple rats!* I missed the ball game.

CORPORAL PUNISHMENT

Later that year during noon recess, over in a far corner of the school grounds a bunch of us boys were playing baseball when someone got a hit that brought in two runs amid a lot of yelling. The bell rang that ended recess during the yelling and none of us heard it. We were so engrossed in the game we did not notice that the rest of the school ground was empty.

A teacher informed the principal that some boys were still playing baseball. A. D. Cleveland, a man with a temper, came out and yelled for us to come in. He directed us to his office where each was to receive one "spat." That was bad news. Those who had received "spats" told of the weapon the principal used. It was a piece of wood about 16 inches long, three inches wide, and two inches thick, with a large hole drilled into it so it would hurt even more.

We followed Mr. Cleveland into the school, dreading the punishment awaiting us. Since the door to the office was next to the fourth grade door, while the other guys dutifully went into the office to receive their punishment, I slipped into my room and took my seat.

Not long after, two or three boys from the group came into our room. One sat across from me who knew I had skipped. "Mr. Cleveland finally believed us that we didn't hear the bell and he let us off this time. We were lucky."

Moments before the closing bell, the school secretary came into our room and whispered something to my teacher. When the bell rang, she said, "Everyone may leave now except Bobby; you wait in your seat." After the other students were gone, she called me to her desk and informed me that the principal wanted to see me right away.

I was caught and scared. I knew I had been missed and that I would be lucky to avoid getting a "spat" even though the other boys were excused from having one. The secretary told me to sit and wait for Mr. Cleveland. He delayed a long time, allowing me to suffer the apprehension of possible terrible things to come. I waited and waited. Finally, the man himself came and stood in his doorway. He looked daggers at me.

"Come in here!" he growled.

"Weren't you one of the boys playing baseball after the bell rang?"

"Yes, Sir."

"Why didn't you come in with the other boys?"

"I was scared!"

"Are you scared now?" he snarled.

"Yes, Sir."

"I let the other boys off because they convinced me they didn't hear the bell. If you had come in with the rest of them, you would not be punished, but since you disobeyed me and went directly to your classroom, I'm going to discipline you." Mr. Cleveland was getting angrier by the minute. He lectured me in gruff tones for disobeying him. He was accustomed to fear and strict obedience. Without them, there were consequences. He opened a drawer and brought out his weapon. I recognized it right away from how others had described it. His eyes flashed and his voice was fearful.

"Get over here and bend over!" I did as he said. All the time he was ranting in angry tones berating me for my failure to obey him. As I bent over, with his hand he smoothed my pants covering my rear end. Then he laid the paddle there. Stupidly, I pretended that this was the spat. I stood up and started to walk out of his office and Mr. Cleveland went berserk. He yelled at me that he was just making sure his aim would be correct. He made me come back, lean over, and he smoothed my pants once again with his hand.

Suddenly, with all his might he hit my behind with force that almost knocked me to the floor. I remember screaming when he hit me. I began sobbing loudly, and Mr. A. D. Cleveland dismissed me from his office. My rear hurt terribly. I was in shock. Fortunately, the school was empty, and I ran down the steps to the basement and into the boys' restroom. For some time I sobbed loudly. I hurt so badly that I could not control my emotions. (I was sore for several days.)

I was alone in the boys' room for a long time. Tears kept rolling from my eyes, and the pain was almost unbearable. I didn't want to go home while I was still crying, so I stayed cooped up in the basement restroom. At long last, my tears stopped falling. I was still in great pain, but the shock had worn off somewhat and I had control of my emotions.

I walked out of the building and went across the schoolyard to the small gymnasium where our eighth graders were playing basketball with eighth graders from another school. I stepped inside long enough to see the players make a couple of baskets, then headed down the sidewalk toward home. When I walked in the house, Mother asked why I was late. "Our school's basketball team is playing another school and I watched them play." True enough, but not the whole truth. I never told a soul about what happened to me until years later. When I told my father, he said he would have gone and talked with A. D. Cleveland, and he added that he may have made a visit to the school superintendent.

BICYCLE SURPRISE

One evening the telephone rang. My sister, Lilian, was in charge since Mom and Dad were out for the evening. The caller, a man who attended our church, asked that I be allowed to come over to his house for a while. He told her he had a gift for me, but Lilian didn't tell me that. She decided to let me go.

The man had always been friendly to me at church, but I didn't know him very well. I walked several blocks to his house and knocked on his front door. He invited me in and said he needed me to help him with a project. I said okay and we went out to his workshop. I saw a large cardboard box that had not been opened. Mr. Goslow took a knife and opened the box. We began taking out wheels, handle bars and other parts of a bicycle. "With your help, Bobby, I think we can put this together." He read the directions, and in an hour or so we had the bicycle assembled.

"It's yours," the kind man said. "I ordered it from the *Sears and Roebuck Catalogu*e just for you." I was speechless. The bike was bright red, my favorite color. The trouble was, I had never ridden a bike before, which I admitted to my benefactor.

"If you'll get up on the seat and take hold of the handle bars and put your feet on the pedals, I'll hold on and help you get started. You should be able to ride all the way home. But if you have a problem, you can get off and walk it home."

"Thank you, thank you," I kept saying. He replied that every boy ought to have a bicycle and he knew my father could not afford to buy me one with his low salary, so he ordered it for me. Later at home we looked in the catalogue and discovered that it cost $39.95, a lot of money in the Depression economy.

Once I got rolling, I kept up the momentum. I knew if I ever stopped, I'd have to walk it the rest of the way home. By this time it was getting dark and the street lights were on. In our small town, there was little traffic at that hour. I slowed down when I came to an intersection, and when I saw no cars coming I pedaled faster. Happily, I made it all the way home without stopping.

Leaving my brand-new bike beside the house would be an invitation to having it stolen. I struggled and got it up the back steps onto our covered back porch. My brother and two sisters came out and were amazed at my beautiful new bike. I soon learned how to get on it and start rolling without help while keeping my balance, and before long, I was a pro. How nice it was to ride back and forth to school each day.

HOBO ALLEY

While we were in Burlington, the Great Depression was at a low point. The jobless rate was more than 20 percent. In the 1930s, traveling homeless men were called "hobos." They went to a train station and waited for a freight train to stop. They crawled into an empty box car and rode to the next town. There they got off and begged for money and food. When they obtained all the freebies they could get, they boarded another empty box car and moved on to the next town.

In many towns, Burlington included, the travelers set up a sort of "hobo camp." There they shared their "take" around a bonfire and slept there overnight. Our house was a short distance from the train tracks, so we had many visitors asking for a handout. My folks never gave money—they had very little of it themselves, but they shared food.

When the number of visitors greatly increased, Dad investigated. Out on the sidewalk someone had made a chalk arrow pointing to our front door. That was a signal to passing hobos that there were possibilities for a handout. Dad used a broom and bucket of water to remove the arrow, but the news still got around.

Our woodpile was out in our back yard where my brother Ed and I took turns chopping for our stoves. Dad came up with the idea of giving a plate of food to anyone who would chop wood for a period of time. Some just walked away, unwilling to do anything to help themselves. Others began chopping, changed their mind, and went on their way. But those who were willing to work the allotted time received a nice meal from my mother.

THE POVERTY LEVEL

If there was an official poverty level, we were way below it. Dad pastored a church where the Sunday morning offering went to the pastor and the Sunday evening offering was designated for church expenses. Most members had little cash, so the offerings were meager.

The members were generous in sharing fruit and vegetables with our family. Mother continued to can produce during the summer. And whenever some farmers slaughtered livestock, they shared meat with us. Mom canned a lot, and we also rented a "locker" in a building downtown. A big room was kept below freezing, and each locker was like a small screened cage we paid so much per month to use. Once in a while, Dad purchased a quarter of beef wrapped for freezing, and the packages were put in the locker properly labeled as roasts, steaks, hamburger, and whatever. We made that meat last a long time.

My uncle operated a "slaughter house," a barn where he bought animals, slaughtered them, prepared the meat, and supplied the town meat markets and grocery stores. Some parts of the cows were not suitable for the markets, so he brought us hearts, tongues, livers, and even "ox tails." The latter were pieces of cow's tail, without the hide with meat in them. My mother made delicious ox-tail stew.

Dad was required to report his income to the church's annual conference each summer. He added up not only Sunday morning offerings, but the market value of the produce and meat members shared with us. I remember one year Dad reported a total income for the year for our family of six as $850. That's an average of $16.35 per week including the gifts of edibles. Likely at least half of the $850 was donated food. Consequently, we didn't eat at restaurants, wear fancy clothes, or go to the store for a five-cent ice cream cone very often.

MY FIRST TRAIN RIDE

Our town of Burlington was five miles north of Mount Vernon, a larger town where we did some of our shopping. We also had a sister church there. We didn't see each other all that often, but certainly did at summer family camp and annual conference.

The Mount Vernon church pastor had three sons, the oldest of which, Keith, married my oldest sister, Lilian. I was good friends with John, Keith's younger brother, who invited me to stay overnight with him. He told me I could ride the train for a nickel.

The passenger train stopped at almost every town, including Burlington and Mount Vernon. At the scheduled time, I boarded the afternoon southbound train, paid my nickel, and a few minutes later got off in Mount Vernon. John was waiting for me and we had a great time together.

I was eleven or twelve and very embarrassed that I still occasionally wet the bed. That happened until my tonsils were removed. That night, sleeping in the same bed with John, I tried to stay awake all night so I wouldn't have an accident. Occasionally I drifted off to sleep in spite of myself. When I awakened, I was terrified. I quickly felt the bed under me.

Fortunately, I had no accident that night. The next day Dad picked me up when he came to Mount Vernon for shopping.

A train ride for five cents! I didn't ride another train for decades, and by that time, the price had gone up considerably.

MY TONSILECTOMY

My throat was often sore, so Dad took me to a doctor in Mount Vernon. When he examined my throat, he was aghast. "This boy's tonsils must be removed!"

The doctor knew Dad could not afford a hospital visit, so he offered to perform the operation in his office after hours. The time came, and I reluctantly laid on a table. The doctor gave me a dose of ether and asked me a question. "Where do you like to swim?" I still remember saying "Snelson's Slue," and then I was out. When I came to, it was dark. I felt weak and had to be helped out to the car. The doctor told my father that my tonsils were so badly infected that if he had known how bad they were he would have insisted on my being hospitalized for the procedure.

Two good things emerged from this experience. First of all, the doctor said the only thing I could swallow for a while was ginger ale mixed with cream. Not half and half. *Cream!* The other good thing was that with all that poison out of my system, I never wet the bed again. Over. Nada. At twelve years of age. Whew! What a relief.

DEALING WITH DEPRESSION

I've never been one to get depressed. But the Great Depression was on and everyone was trying to scratch out a living. The U.S. Congress passed two pieces of legislation that met part of the need.

An act of Congress created the CCC—Civilian Conservation Corps. It involved young men ages 19-25 who were unemployed. CCC camps were located where work projects were planned. My brother Ed was in CCC for a year after high school before he went on to college. He was given room and board and a small allowance. The rest was sent to our parents to help with family expenses.

Another act of Congress created the WPA (Works Progress Administration). This was mostly for unemployed men, involving them in building roads, working in national parks, etc. One man in our church knew how to use dynamite, so he was employed by WPA as a "blaster." They built roads along the sides of hills where he set the dynamite to dislodge and break up rock formations to make room for the roads. WPA also subsidized dentists, and since we were dirt poor, we received free dental care.

TROMBONE TRAGEDY

WPA did something else that sounded great. At school, we were told we could receive free musical instrument lessons from a teacher paid by WPA. I went to the teacher who showed me several instruments. I was enchanted by the sliding trombone. I said, "I would like to take lessons on this one."

"Good for you, young man. All you have to do is get your own trombone and your lessons won't cost you a thing."

When I got home that afternoon, I was on a high. I announced to my family, "I'm going to get free lessons on the trombone at school." Everyone was happy for me. "The only thing is," I added, "I have to have a trombone of my own." *Silence.* "Mom, Dad, I need to buy a trombone. Can you take me to Mount Vernon to the music store where they have new and used ones?" Dad explained that we couldn't afford one.

"Can't we pay for it a little at a time?"

"We don't have the money."

To my shame, I cried and begged for a considerable time. Then my sister, Lilian, took me aside. "Do you know Mom is in her bedroom crying because the folks can't afford a trombone?" That put me to shame. I hushed and went to my room.

Fast forward to when I had a daughter in junior high school. She came to me and said, "Dad, can I get a trombone?"

"You bet!" We could afford both the instrument and the lessons. The Great Depression was history. My dream was lived out as Karis became first chair trombonist in both the high school orchestra and the jazz band.

Now for the rest of the story. A few days later, after things quieted down over my tirade about wanting a trombone, Dad said, "Son, you're old enough to have an allowance. We're giving you twenty-five cents per week. That will pay for your piano lessons. I've arranged for you to take lessons from Mrs. Simmons. She lives near your school and you can go to her house from school one afternoon a week. You can practice at home on our piano." That explains why I play the piano rather than a trombone.

PICKING STRAWBERRIES

When I was in fifth grade, I began summer employment. Burlington lies in the rich Skagit Valley in the northwest corner of the state of Washington, where strawberries are one of the major crops.

My sister, Irene, and I signed on to pick strawberries, kneeling in the hot sand on summer days. I did that for three summers. One spring the crop came in early and those of us who could bring a note to school proving that we had a job picking berries got out of school a week early. We picked the ripe berries and put them in quart-sized boxes in a carrier. Our pay was slightly over one cent per quart, or twenty-five cents for a tray of 24 quarts. And if we stayed through the end of the season without leaving when the picking became sparse, we received a bonus of five cents for each tray.

When we were paid at the end of the picking season, I remember proudly taking home my summer earnings and giving them to Dad for safe keeping. According to our practice, I gave 10 percent to the church. As school neared, Mother asked me if I would like to spend my strawberry money for school clothes. I knew our financial situation, so I agreed. We went to Mount Vernon to J.C. Penney where I was able to pay for pants, shirts, shoes, socks, and underclothes. Mother told me she was proud of me, and to tell you the truth, so was I.

STRAWBERRY FESTIVAL

I mentioned earlier that the sign coming into town said, Burlington: Population 1,407. But every summer, when the town sponsored a strawberry festival with carnival rides, our town was choked with thousands of people.

One of the features each year was "The world's largest strawberry shortcake." The town bakery made shortcakes and placed them side by side completely covering a flatbed truck. Strawberry growers furnished the berries and the bakery did the rest. Eating was free.

SUPER SALESMAN

When I was in fifth grade, I saw in the back of one of my mother's women's magazines an advertisement that you could earn a prize by selling Burpee Seeds. I asked my folks, and they encouraged me to go for it.

I clipped out the order blank and mailed it in. Soon a box was delivered with a large number of packets of vegetable and flower seeds. I started out right away going from door to door selling the seeds. During the Depression, almost everyone raised a garden. Before long I had sold every packet of seeds in the box. Dad deposited the money in the bank and wrote a check to Burpee Seeds. Now the fun began. Along with the seeds came a catalogue of things I could receive free for selling the entire contents of the box. Mother was interested, too, and looked over the items. I had three or four toys and things I was interested in when Mother made a suggestion.

"You know, Bobby, that you need a new blanket for your bed. Here is one you can order." In due time, the blanket arrived in the mail. This was another time Mother said she was proud of me. And once again, so was I when I snuggled under my warm blanket.

THE WATERMELON DISASTER

One Saturday, some friends from out of town dropped in for a visit in late morning, and Mother invited them to stay for lunch. The visitors were embarrassed that they were making this imposition on my mother, and politely declined, saying they would move on. But Mother insisted they stay.

"Can we help in any way?" they asked. The father said, "We could run over to the store and get a watermelon." Mother agreed that would be a good idea.

"Bobby, you go with them in the car and direct them to the store." I climbed in the car and off we went. The gentleman picked out the biggest watermelon he could find and paid for it.

"I'll carry it out to the car," I boasted.

"Isn't that too heavy for you?"

"No, I can handle it."

I picked up the big bruiser and headed for the car. As I stepped through the doorway and onto the sidewalk, I tripped and lost my grip. Down went the watermelon, splattering in juicy pieces all over the sidewalk. You can't imagine how I felt. I was mortified. "I'm so sorry! I'm so sorry!" I kept repeating. Our visitor assured me it was okay and returned into the store and bought another large watermelon. This time he carried it out to the car. As we sat eating lunch, I felt like I was six inches tall.

THE DAY A MOUSE BECAME A RAT

Our house featured a covered back porch and a storage/work room. To save money, Dad bought large bags of flour, oatmeal, and other cooking needs and kept them in the storage room. The bag of oatmeal was sitting on the work bench.

Dad went out to the room and found that a mouse had chewed a hole in the oatmeal bag and helped himself. Immediately, Dad set a mouse trap with cheese as bait. The next morning, the mousetrap was sprung, the cheese was gone, and so was more of our oatmeal. *I'll take care of this critter*, Dad thought. He set *three* mousetraps on the work bench. The next morning, all three were sprung, and there lay a stunned rat, still alive. With a piece of wood, Dad made sure there was no more stealing from our oatmeal bag.

ROOF, ROOF!

Needing to put food on our table, my dad occasionally contracted to re-roof a house or other building. For example, he installed a new roof on a school. He carried a shovel up on the roof, ripped off the old shingles, then lifted heavy bundles of shingles up the ladder and nailed them on.

My job was to gather up the mess of old shingles, many with nails still in them, and pile them where a truck could pick up the trash for the garbage dump. I almost never got on a roof since I have always had a problem with height. I guess you might call it a phobia, so I stayed on the ground.

One time Dad contracted to replace the roof of First Church in Seattle. It was a large old wood-framed building with a steep slanting roof. In fact, there were several smaller steep roofs built in as well, including on top of the church's bell tower. How he did it I cannot imagine. I was not with him for that job. One way or another, he managed to keep us fed and healthy. Dad's roof business on the side also helped us buy clothing and meet other needs we could not otherwise have afforded.

SEEING A GHOST

One hot summer afternoon I wandered lazily around our shaded yard. I lay on my back in the grass and watched the clouds. I could see changing shapes of the clouds including faces and other formations. Tiring of that, I strolled down the sidewalk along the side of the church. Something caught my attention. There on the white wood siding of the building I saw wavy shadows moving from the bottom of the building up the side. I thought I was seeing a ghost.

Dad happened to be home and I ran into the house to get him. "Dad, I think I see a ghost out on the side of the church!" He laid his hand on my shoulder and I led him to the spot. "That's not a ghost," he said. "Those are heated molecules in the air rising from the hot pavement. Put your hand down and see how hot it is." I did and it was very hot.

"I don't understand what you mean."

Patiently, Dad explained that when air is heated to an extreme level, the molecules become agitated. Since heat rises, the molecules rising in the air from the sidewalk are thick enough to cast a shadow. I didn't understand how "thin air" could become thick enough to cast a shadow, but I figured my Dad knew what he was talking about. That was a first-rate science lesson, a really hot topic.

So much for ghosts!

CHORES GALORE

In our family of six, everyone had duties to perform. In Burlington I recall quite a range of things I was assigned to do. Outside the house, it was my job to mow the lawn around the church and parsonage. On hot summer days, that was a pain. I used an old push mower, so the power had to come from my muscles. The church expected the pastor's family to do this and other tasks for free.

Every spring I was involved in digging up the garden plot in our back yard, quite a large area. Then came hoeing, breaking up the clods of dirt, and smoothing out the surface with a rake. Next we planted the seeds. As the veggies began to grow, it was also my responsibility to get rid of the weeds with a hoe so the veggies would not have to share the nutrients of the soil with them.

The men of our church went out into the woods during the summer, cut down trees, and trimmed off the branches. My job was helping with the trimming. A truck hauled the trees to the area behind the church. A rented "buzz saw" on wheels was pulled behind a vehicle to where the trees were lying. The trees were "buzzed" into longer lengths for the church's wood furnace, and into shorter lengths for the parsonage stoves. All the wood ended up as round sections of a log. It was up to my brother Ed and me to split the wood into sizes that would dry out and burn easily. That's one way I developed my muscles.

Inside the house were other duties, like doing dishes. Yes, we had an automatic dishwasher in those days—me! And, of course, my sister, Irene. Supper dishes, silverware, and pots and pans were our responsibility. We took turns washing, drying, and putting everything away where it belonged. That was a ritual every evening. On Saturday, the family was organized to clean the linoleum floors, wash windows, dust the furniture, etc. No one was left behind, and believe me, we all worked together. And too, we made our own beds each morning, which wasn't my favorite thing to do.

MARIAN THE LIBRARIAN

The task I enjoyed most was keeping my mother supplied with books from the library. She was a voracious reader, and selected many series of books to read. For example, over a period of time she read every book in the library about Abraham Lincoln. She became fascinated with the Czars of Russia, and read all the books on Russian history. Someone told Mom about Zane Grey's western novels and she read them all.

I learned the layout of the library quite well, but sometimes could not find what Mom wanted. That's when I approached "Marian the Librarian" who knew where everything was located in the building. She was always nice about helping me find what mother wanted.

Happily, mother's love for books rubbed off on me. I read a series of novels about a boy whose name I cannot remember. One book I remember reading was *The Yearling* by Rawlins. In my imagination I could "see" the story as it unfolded. Many years later, I saw the movie version. "They got it all wrong!" I protested. What I saw on the screen was not the same as I remembered on the screen of my imagination.

Thanks, Mom. I still love to read.

WAR OF THE WORLDS

Two startling things happened while we lived in Burlington. The most startling was a Sunday-afternoon radio program by Orson Wells, the actor and film maker. In the program, weird-looking aliens from Mars invaded New York City and were headed for all parts of our country. Their goal was to wipe out the human race and colonize our planet. They arrived in strange space vehicles. The format, without commercials, involved live reporters describing what was happening as streets were jammed with cars trying to get out of New York City.

Thousands of people believed it was true, and panic spread across the country. While the program continued, one family in our church drove up into a mountain area where they thought they would be safe. It turned out to be a fictitious drama, but it shook our nation to its foundations that fateful Sunday afternoon.

HOUSE ON FIRE

Another startling thing happened when a neighbor rushed over and banged loudly on our front door. Dad opened the door and the woman shouted, *"Your house is on fire."* Dad rushed through the house telling everyone to get out. After we ran outside, we could see flames coming from the chimney. Dad called the fire department and they doused the flames.

When the fire was out, the firemen told my dad he should hire a chimney cleaner to do a thorough cleaning. Dad did that and there were no more fires.

WRITING A BOOK

Besides enjoying reading, I also liked to write. In fifth grade, my teacher had an idea for an English project. He suggested that our class write a book about Paul Bunyon. Students were assigned to write one chapter using their imagination. After reading the original story of Paul Bunyon and his blue ox, my imagination took over. I wrote my chapter, but I don't remember what it contained. The teacher put all our chapters together, creating a hand-written class book.

Today, with computers and copy machines, we would all receive a copy, but not then. I'd give a hundred dollars to get my hands on that book about Paul Bunyon that our class wrote.

AN ANGRY TEACHER

My fifth-grade teacher was a Dutchman. Dutch people have a reputation for being strong-minded. One of my fellow students was the son of the school superintendent who thought this made him immune from any of the rules of the school or classroom. This did not work out very well with our teacher.

"Mr. Dutchman" was writing on the blackboard while we were supposed to be quietly doing handwork at our desks. The superintendent's son got out of line and the teacher gave him his orders, but nothing changed. Finally, the boy spoke up and said, "Are you forgetting I'm the superintendent's son?" With that, the teacher snapped. Since he had been writing on the blackboard, he had a piece of chalk in his hand, and in a fit of anger threw it at the boy. "I'm going to tell my dad!" And he did. When the teacher came to school the following morning, he was met by the superintendent. When class started, our teacher humbly apologized to his boss's son for throwing the chalk at him. The next year, Mr. Dutchman was no longer a teacher at Lincoln Grade School.

PADDLE DEE DEE

When I was in school, corporal punishment was not only allowed, but encouraged. Our principal used such tactics, and so did some of our teachers. My sixth-grade teacher demanded strict obedience in her classroom. The penalty for disobedience was kept in her desk drawer, a piece of plywood cut into the shape of a hand and wrist.

When she used it, she would have the student hold out his or her hand, fingers together and flat. To help, she held the student's wrist and pressed down on the fingers to show what she meant by flat. In one swift motion she whacked the student's hand as hard as she could with the wooden hand. I'll have to "hand" it to her; it was a pretty effective way of controlling her class. She gave one warning, then for a second offence she administered a *Whack!*

I got through most of the year without receiving a whack. Then my turn came. We had penmanship the last period of the day. Our desks each had an ink well and an old-fashioned pen. The pen had a long, tapered wooden handle, and the pen "head" was metal and came to a sharp point. We dipped the pen in an ink well and wrote with it.

In penmanship class we wrote long rows of circles in coiled form trying to keep them round and the same size. Another "exercise" was to make a long row of vertical lines. This was designed to help us with our cursive writing. I finished the assignment and was sitting quietly at my desk waiting for the bell. I took the pen and dropped is onto the porous worn wooden floor. It stuck in the floor while the handle wiggled back and forth until it stopped. I kept doing that until the closing bell rang.

Our teacher said, "You're all dismissed except Bob Haslam." Instinctively I knew what was happening. She had seen me dropping the pen and didn't like it. She called me to her desk and said, "Hold out your hand—*flat!*" I did as she said. As the wooden hand headed down toward my hand, without meaning to my hand instinctively "cupped" and she hit the rim all the way around.

"Let's try that again," she said. "Keep your hand flat this time or we'll do it again." This time I was able to keep my hand flat. *Whack! Ouch!* My hand became numb and filled with pain. I never dropped the pen again.

One kid who got whacked quite often walked to school, so didn't have to catch a bus. One afternoon after school was out, he went into the boy's restroom in the basement and waited until he figured the teachers were gone. Then he climbed the stairs to the second floor, opened our teacher's desk drawer, and removed the wooden hand. He slipped it inside his shirt and got rid of it by taking it to the basement and putting it in the coal-fired furnace. At that time of day there was a bed of embers and the dry wood caught fire immediately.

Our teacher ranted and raved the next day demanding that whoever stole her wooden hand confess. No one did, but we all knew the secret. For many days, he was "king of the mountain."

NECK MASSAGE

While I'm on the subject of corporal punishment, let's move on to seventh grade. Our teacher was a man who also demanded obedience in his classroom. He gave us an assignment to do at our desks while he sat at his desk in front of the class. I suppose he was grading papers, but he always maintained awareness of what was going on.

I had the misfortune of sitting across from the superintendent's son, the one who got the Dutchman fired. He and I both had seats at the rear end of our rows. He didn't think rules applied to him, so he looked my way and whispered something. Our teacher cleared his throat and said, "No whispering, please." This jerk kept whispering to me. I responded by whispering, "Hush, or we'll get in trouble." Just then the teacher looked our way. Oops! We were both implicated.

Quietly, Mr. Teacher Man rose from his desk and started walking around the perimeter of the room. As he approached, we were busy working at our desks. Suddenly he grasped the back of each of our necks and pinched with all his might. It was excruciating.

Unfortunately, he had me by his right hand. He held us a long time with a firm grip. His act damaged my neck and it hurt for many days. Without a word, he released his hold and returned to his desk.

The superintendent's son sitting next to me whispered, "I'm going to tell my dad." We moved to another town that summer, but I speculate that Mr. Teacher Man was not re-hired the following year.

Face In the Sawdust

When I was in the sixth grade, one day on the playground a boy named John told me he was trying to persuade a girl to be his girlfriend. I began to kid him and he became furious. He chased me shouting threats. I got behind the baseball screened backstop. When he went one way, I dashed the other. Then he tricked me. He started to go one way and I went the other. Only he quickly reversed his direction and met me at the end of the backstop.

John grabbed me (he was older and stronger than I was) and dragged me over to where the long jump was set up.

It was filled with sawdust so that when the long jumper landed, it would not be such a jolt. John grabbed my hair, pushed me down, and rubbed my face in the sawdust. After he worked out his rage and let me come up for air, my mouth, nose, and eyes were filled with sawdust.

"There! That will teach you to mess with me!" he shouted. I sat on the ground, took out my handkerchief, and cleaned up the mess on my face. I never bothered John again.

GOTTA BE PERFECT
During a recess, one of my classmates asked me, "Is your dad a male man?"

"No," I replied.

"What is he, a female man?"

He tricked me. I thought he said mail man, but it was really male man.

Then he asked me, "What does your dad do?"

"My dad is a preacher. He pastors the church over by the high school."

My friend frowned. "So you're the son of preacher. That means *you've gotta be perfect!"* I cringed at the thought; I knew I wasn't perfect. Suddenly I realized that kids who knew my father was a preacher held me to a higher standard than for themselves. That was uncomfortable. It haunted me for years. I felt that I didn't belong, like a speckled bird, an ugly duckling. It took me years to overcome that feeling of inferiority. I found it difficult to feel that I was equal with my peers.

NATIONAL WINNERS
We regularly received *The Weekly Reader*. For one thing, it was created to foster interest in reading, carrying features from other schools and around the world. One year the *Weekly Reader* sponsored a national contest for all elementary schools. It was about cleaning up and beautifying the

school property. Our sixth-grade class decided to enter the competition.

We brought rakes and hoes to school and cleaned up the entire school grounds. However, we first took pictures to show how shabby our grounds were. We also planted flowers and small shrubs in strategic places. Over against the small school gymnasium stood a rickety and partially-broken bike rack. With the advice and direction of parents, we tore it out and built a new one. When we were finished we took pictures that showed the improvement over the previous photos. We wrote up what we had done, enclosed the photos, and sent them in.

In due time, *The Weekly Reader* produced an issue that awarded first, second, and third prizes for school improvement. Out of hundreds, maybe thousands of entrants, we won second place in the national contest. What a day of rejoicing that was!

TIMES OF TEMPTATION

THE TREE HOUSE

From the time I began school, Dad talked with me about boy-girl relationships. He taught me to respect girls and not think of them as sex objects. He urged me to have a mindset that I would never have sex until I married. In Burlington, this was sorely tested.

A guy in my class got me off alone on the school grounds and asked me if I had ever had sex with a girl. I said I had not. "It's wonderful!" he exulted. "You really ought to try it." He went on to say that his dad had built him a big tree house well away from their farm home. After school some days a few boys and girls climbed into the tree house and took turns having sex. He invited me to go home with him on the bus and stay overnight. In the afternoon he would see that I had opportunity to be with a girl in the tree house.

I stumbled for words and told him weakly that my parents would not approve of that. "Forget it. My parents don't know. Your parents don't need to know, either." Finally, I told him what my father had taught me, and that I didn't plan to do anything like that before I married. Surprisingly, my friend didn't try to persuade me further. He seemed to respect what I said.

THE CUTE GIRL

After I got my bicycle, I rode to school and back. It happened that a cute girl lived on a farm on the edge of town. Often as I rode home she took the same route I did until she made a right turn to go to her place. Suzy, I'll call her, began timing her ride home to coincide with mine. We rode along and talked about what happened at school that day. She told me her dad owned a farm and asked what my father did. I told her, and soon she began riding her bike to our church Sunday mornings. I could tell she liked me, and I liked her, too.

One afternoon when we came to her turnoff, she said, "Why don't you ride with me to my place? We can go to the barn, climb into the hayloft, and have some fun. Instinctively, I knew what she meant by "fun." I told her my mother was expecting me home any minute, so went on. For several days, she kept inviting me. Finally I began taking a different route home. I could have…, but thanks to my upbringing, I was able to withstand the temptation. Suzy soon stopped attending our church.

THE PROPOSITION

Another time at school I was with a boy during recess who asked me if I had ever had sex with a girl. I replied that I hadn't. He went on and on telling me how much fun it was. Then he made a proposition. "If you'll go home with me on the bus to our farm and stay overnight, I can work something out for you. I have two sisters, and both of them

78

enjoy entertaining boys. One of them can go with you up into the hayloft and initiate you." For farm kids, the hayloft was where lots of things happened, especially sexual exploits. By then I knew about it. When I declined, he questioned me and I blamed my folks, but really I knew I wanted to stay true to my own principles. Thanks to the careful teaching of my father, when I married at the age of 25, I had saved myself for my bride—and she for me.

THE TOWN ATHEIST

I had a friend at school named Ken. His father was a brother of two members of my dad's church, but he was an atheist. He had been in the armed services and contracted an exotic disease, perhaps in a tropical land. No one with this disease normally lived more than three months, but Sam (I'll call him) lived with it for several years. Leading medical specialists flew from the East Coast to the state of Washington to examine him. His case was written up more than once in medical journals as a baffling case of survival of the dread disease.

Sam's brother and sister cautioned my dad not to try to contact him. Previous preachers tried, and Sam cursed them off his property. He was an atheist and intended to stay that way. This man was known by everyone in town. He frequented the town's bar down by the railroad where he proclaimed his atheistic beliefs. The word spread that Sam's strange illness was taking its toll and he was going downhill physically. Dad heard the sad news and was concerned about Sam. He prayed a great deal and felt that he should take the risk and visit him. When he knocked on the door, Sam's wife responded.

"Is Sam here?"

"Yes he is, but he's sick in bed. And who may I ask are you?"

"I'm Pastor Oliver Haslam."

Sam's wife drew back. "Oh, you can't come in. Sam is not well."

"But I must see him," Dad insisted.

Reluctantly, she let him in and led him to Sam's bedroom. When Dad walked in, the radio was on with a Seattle baseball game. "What's the score?" Dad asked. Instantly, the two men began talking baseball. Dad knew the name and position of every member of the Seattle team. He knew all their batting averages and was an avid baseball fan; so was Sam. When the game ended, Dad thanked Sam for letting him hear the game. He left saying, "I hope you get better, Sam."

Dad developed a strategy. He visited the sick man only when a Seattle baseball game was on the radio. They became fast friends, even though Sam knew Dad was a preacher. It was a unique relationship in which Dad never brought up the subject of religion.

One evening when Dad went to visit Sam, his wife, with tears, said that her husband was getting very low. She was afraid he was nearing death. That night when the game ended, Sam turned off the radio. Dad simply asked, "Sam, may I say a prayer for you?"

"Sure, preacher."

Dad prayed a simple prayer asking the Lord to have his hand upon Sam, and then he left, but with a heavy heart. He longed to talk with Sam about getting right with God, but the man would have to open that door himself.

A day or two later, Sam's wife called Dad and said Sam wanted him to bring the midweek prayer service to his house, and be sure that Mrs. Nelson came along. Dad spread the word by telephone. I was there that night when people from our church crowded into the living room. The kids sat on the floor, as there weren't enough seats for everyone. Sam sat in a rocking chair wrapped in a blanket. He requested one old hymn after another to be sung. Then he looked at Mrs. Nelson and said, "The last time I was in your church, as I was about to go out the door you told me you were praying for me. I cursed you under my breath when I was still in the church. That has bothered me for years. Will you please forgive me?" Mrs. Nelson tearfully said she did.

Sam had been raised in a Christian home. His sister told Dad that Sam's father literally died praying for his son. Sam could never forget that fact. "Rev. Haslam, pray for me that I can get right with God." Dad went over, laid his hand on Sam's shoulder and prayed a simple prayer. With tears streaming down his face, Sam looked up and told the assembled group that Jesus had come into his heart, forgiven him of his sins, and given him peace.

The next Sunday, Sam came to church, carried in a rocking chair to the front of the sanctuary. (We didn't have a wheel chair available.) That morning, the former town atheist joined the church. There wasn't a dry eye in the building. Within a few days, Sam came back to church, this time in a casket. Everyone who was anyone in Burlington was there, the town officials, Sam's drinking buddies, and many more. In his sermon, Dad told the remarkable story of Sam's conversion from atheism to faith in Jesus Christ as his Savior.

I've always admired my father for his courage and wisdom in approaching Sam, befriending him, and helping him prepare to meet his Maker.

CHAPTER FIVE:
Betrayal

Dad and Bob gathering wood in Burien

After school on a sunny day

All dressed up under a cherry tree

*"Grow in the grace and knowledge
of our Lord and Savior Jesus Christ."*
(2 Peter 3:18)

ANOTHER MAJOR TRANSITION

S uch is the life of a preacher's kid. Born in the big city of Seattle, followed by four years in the small lumber town of National, three years in the concrete jungle of the capital city of Olympia, then four more in the country town of Burlington, only to land next in a suburb of the city of my birth. Every place possessed its own unique atmosphere. You never know what to expect when you're a preacher's kid.

We moved to the suburb of Burien in August of 1941. On December 7, the Japanese attacked Pearl Harbor and we were quickly enveloped in the Greater Seattle wartime way of life.

Our government suspected that the Japanese navy might attack our West Coast. Since Seattle housed Boeing Aircraft Company that produced several bombers each day for the war effort, defensive preparations were made throughout the city in the event of a Japanese air attack. Ship building was located in nearby Bremerton.

Every home was instructed to have window shades that would not reveal light at night. We were advised to stay in at night, not drive, not light a match or use a flashlight outdoors. A small light can be seen from the air and it was thought an air attack from a Japanese aircraft carrier might occur at night. We had what were called "blackouts."

Each evening at dusk, giant fingers of light from searchlights pierced the sky. Whenever a plane flew over Seattle after dark, it was caught in the glare of many searchlights as they followed it across the sky. Those manning the searchlights were familiar with every type of American and Japanese airplane. Anti-aircraft units were scattered in and around the city to defend against foreign intruders. I often went out in our yard at night and watched as planes crossed the sky reflecting the brilliance of the powerful searchlights. In bed at night, I dreaded the thought of planes bombing us. Whenever I heard a plane overhead, I prayed for our safety.

Surrounding the Boeing Aircraft factory were military emplacements. From them helium balloons rose high into the sky with lengthy heavy metal chains dangling to catch in the propellers of planes that might fly in at low altitudes for an attack. One of the balloon emplacements was located not far from where we lived, and a soldier from that operation attended our church.

The Boeing factory was located alongside a stream. Should enemy planes come in by day with maps of the city, they could easily locate the factory beside the stream. To counteract such a possibility, an elaborate means was made to disguise the factory. Tall poles were erected all around and over the factory and netting was stretched from pole to pole. The netting was the color of grass. In certain places, the empty skeletons of small farm buildings were atop the nets, supported by poles. The netting also covered the stream so that pilots, looking for the target would be confused.

Rationing was initiated by the government. We needed government-issued books of coupons to buy all kinds of meat, except for chicken. Other books were designated for gasoline. My father was allowed more than the average gasoline coupons because he was a pastor.

Priority was also given to those who worked in wartime factories.

AN UNTHINKABLE TRAGEDY

As the war got under way, the government was concerned about the thousands of Japanese people, many of them American citizens, who lived on the West Coast. Officials worried that they would leak information to the enemy that would enable them to attack our country more effectively. Thus, all people of Japanese ancestry in West Coast states, including American citizens, were forced to leave their homes and businesses and relocate to internment camps.

In Highline High School, dozens of students were of Japanese ancestry. Some of the boys were star baseball players on our school team, while others were student body officers. All were good students making high grades. An assembly was held when we said farewell to our Japanese friends who were being treated as enemy spies by our government. If this happened in the 1960s, it would have started a riot. Instead, we tearfully told them good-bye. There wasn't a dry eye in the auditorium. I still remember the feeling of injustice that day in our fateful assembly.

Many decades later, our government admitted that their confinement was unconstitutional and paid reparations to those still living who had been in the camps. I'm sure my friends were among them.

WAR COMES TO WASHINGTON

My father received a letter from the government asking him to read it in church on Sunday morning and then destroy the letter. It told that Japanese armed forces were sending balloons high in the air that came across the Pacific Ocean on the jet stream that circles the globe. They estimated how long it would take the balloons to cross the Pacific and reach Seattle, and armed them with a timing device to determine when the balloons descended to the ground. Each balloon was attached to a small incendiary device that would burst into flame upon landing. These were aimed for Seattle.

The Japanese miscalculated the timing and the balloons flew beyond their target over the Cascade Mountains to Eastern Washington and Idaho where they started fires in the ripening grain fields. The government was afraid to publish a warning in newspapers, fearing spies among us. Thus pastors were asked to inform their congregations not to approach any suspicious object, but call the police and be prepared to call the fire department should one land on your house's roof and start a fire.

In the letter was the story that one balloon bomb had landed in a lake in Oregon. A family was out boating and a boy saw an object in the water, reached out, picked it up, and it exploded into flame. The boy died, perhaps the only war casualty in the continental United States.

WHOSE SIDE ARE YOU ON?

My parents had been missionaries in Japan several years before I was born. This became known at Highline High School and my father was asked to come speak to the students about Japan. Dad talked about the culture and the land, then gave the students opportunity to ask questions. Someone piped up and asked him, "Whose side are you on in this war?" Dad assured the students he was a loyal American and regretted the secret attack by the Japanese at Pearl Harbor.

MADE IN JAPAN

My brother, Ed, was working at Boeing when the Second World War began with the attack on Pearl Harbor. Sometime after the war started, Ed was called aside for consultation. He was informed that the government required war industries to check the birth records of all employees. They noted the fact that he was born in Japan, and requested his birth certificate.

Ed explained that he was the son of missionaries to Japan and was born in that country on Awagi Island. He went home and asked Dad for his birth certificate, but Dad replied he had not been given one. The personnel department at Boeing was not satisfied. "You must produce documentation of your birth or lose your job." With the war going on, no contact could be made with anyone in Japan.

Dad had an inspiration. He remembered sending a telegram from Japan to the mission headquarters in America informing them of Ed's birth. He wrote a letter asking for a search of their records to see if it could be located. Fortunately, it had been preserved in my father's file. This was mailed to Dad and the matter was resolved.

Following the conclusion of the war, Dad returned to Japan to help the Japanese church after the devastation of wartime bombing raids. While there, he visited Awagi Island and amazingly located the elderly doctor who had presided over Ed's birth twenty-some years earlier. He was able to obtain an authentic birth certificate for Ed at last.

HIRED OUT AS A FARM HAND

During the war, farm life went on. I had always loved farms. At my father's churches I occasionally went home Sunday afternoon with a farm family and roamed the farm during the afternoon. I enjoyed the freedom, the animals, and the out-of-doors, and thought a farm was about the best place on earth.

After we moved to Burien from Burlington, my sister, Irene, kept in touch with one of her former school friends who had graduated and immediately married her high school sweetheart. His father gave him the responsibility of running one of his farms, and Irene's friend said they needed a farm hand. Irene told me about this, and I asked my parents what they thought of letting me work on a farm for the summer. This was when I was fourteen. My folks said yes, and after an exchange of letters, I was hired and Dad drove me sixty miles north of Seattle to the farm. Mom made me promise to write faithfully.

Was I ever in for a surprise! The first evening, I was told to set my alarm for 4:30 a.m. to go out in the fields and bring in the cows. Before long, the cows recognized my voice and responded when I called. They filed into the barn and into the stalls. I put feed in the trough, and while they ate I went from stall to stall and closed the gate so the cows could not back out of them. Then came the milking. After milking, we went in for breakfast, and then I went back out to the barn, opened the gates, and the cows went out to pasture. That was when the worst part occurred. Using a flat shovel, I filled it with the cows' leavings and took it out to the manure pile. This required several trips. I've never had a stinkier job.

During the heat of the day, I had two major jobs. One was splitting wood for the kitchen stove and the wood-burning heater to keep till the weather grew cool in the fall. I already had plenty of practice splitting wood, so that was not a problem. However, doing it in the heat of the sun was not much fun. My other task was weeding the garden. The couple had planted a large garden in the spring, and the plants were coming up; so were the weeds. I was given a hoe and told to weed the garden between the rows of vegetables. Under the blazing summer sun, I got hot, sweaty, and tired. When I wasn't hoeing, I chopped wood.

Soon the mail brought a letter from my mother asking me how things were going, but I still had more to do. In late afternoon I went out to the pasture and called the cows back in. I followed the same procedure as in the morning, then the milking, and supper followed. After that, back out to let the cows out of the barn and get rid of the stinking manure; then my day's work was done. By then, I was tired, and after my bath, I didn't linger long before going to bed. We had no TV—nothing. I knew I had to get up again at 4:30 the next morning.

After a few days, this routine got old. The young newlywed couple, other than milking cows and meal time, spent their time upstairs. I was alone downstairs in the big old farmhouse in the evening. Because of my routine and fatigue at the end of the day, I never started correspondence with my mother. After two weeks, a letter came from her- -"*Come home.*" Dad drove up and brought me home. My love affair with farm living was over.

MY FIFTEENTH SUMMER

Highline High School was eighth grade through twelfth. Grades eight and nine were junior high. After completing grade nine, I was fifteen. Knowing my folks could not afford to send me to college, I wanted to work and save money for that purpose. Some guys at school arranged to work at Boeing Aircraft during the summer, so I applied. However, I was told the government policy for producing wartime airplanes required employees to be at least sixteen. Bummer.

Someone told me that downtown Seattle was a good place to find summer work. They suggested I try the Virginia Street Market. I went downtown and ventured from one vender to another in the market. When I asked if they needed help in the meat market, the owner said he did, and hired me on the spot. Six days each week I took the bus downtown, worked all day, then rode another bus home. I learned every cut of meat and how to cut up chickens. Since meat was rationed, people were required to have ration books and tokens, as well as money.

One experience that summer revealed a glimpse into shady business practices. Pork chops in the cooling room were turning green with mold. I told my boss and he instructed me to scrape the green off. He got on the phone to a nearby hotel and arranged to sell them to the chef. I scraped and washed until the mold disappeared. Then I was told to wrap them in butcher paper and deliver them to the chef at the hotel. I did this in obedience to an order, but was worried that the meat might make people sick. My boss told me, "Don't worry. The cook will prepare it in such a way that no one will ever suspect what we've done." I felt guilty, but didn't have the authority to question my boss.

Saturdays were a nightmare for me. Since chickens were not rationed, everybody and their dog came in to buy chickens on Saturday for Sunday dinner. I was commissioned to be the chicken guy on Saturdays. Late in the week, our boss purchased a large number of whole chickens. Their feathers were off, but their innards were still in them. We placed several large tubs in the cooling room filled with water and chunks of ice to keep the chickens fresh. When people lined up, they told me how many chickens they wanted, and I fetched them from the cooling room. For those who planned to bake their chicken, it remained whole. However, I had to clean out the innards. Some wanted to keep the organ meat (heart, liver, and gizzard) and others did not. When they didn't want them, I put it those parts in a container and took them home with my boss's permission. Many people asked for their chickens to be cut up, and I took them directly out of ice water. Pulling out the innards got my hands the coldest, but even in cutting up the chickens, they were ice cold. Over a period of hours of doing this, my hands were numb from the effects of ice water.

When summer was over, I was asked to come in on Saturdays and be the chicken guy. I did this throughout the fall months. I was able to save most of my money for college, although I had the expense of bus fare to take out of my profits. I also gave ten percent to the church.

MY CHURCH JANITOR JOB
For the three years we were in Burien, I filled the role of church janitor, but cleaning the building was only part of the deal. During cold weather I got up Sunday mornings no later than 5:00 a.m. and lit the fire in the church furnace. On Saturday evening, I put in paper, kindling, small wood, then larger wood. On Sunday morning I lit the paper with a match and made sure the kindling and wood burned well enough to warm the building.

But where did that wood come from? One year it came from a wooded area. Another year Dad and I passed a location where they were bulldozing trees to make room for houses. Dad stopped and asked if we could have the wood for the church. We could, but we had to hurry and get the trees out of their way. Men from the church joined Dad and me in trimming off the limbs and sawing the logs into lengths that would fit on the back of a truck. We hauled them to the church. A buzz saw was towed in and the wood was cut both into longer lengths for the church furnace and shorter ones for the parsonage stoves.

Like Abraham Lincoln, I was a "rail splitter," splitting each section into sizes to burn in the stoves and furnace. When I came home from school, I headed for the woodpile. The church paid me for cleaning the church, heating it properly, mowing the lawn, and cutting the wood. This was at the beginning of the end of the Great Depression, and my pay was $5.00—*per month*. I gave fifty cents to the church, and $4.50 went toward my college fund.

CHRISTMAS SALES

My father found a line of boxed Christmas cards that were especially beautiful with 24 different cards in each box. He said that in my spare time I could go up and down the streets, knock on doors, and take orders. From the beginning people oohed and ahed over the cards—they practically sold themselves. I took orders during fall months and delivered them to my customers in plenty of time to mail their cards before Christmas.

Dad was delighted with how many orders I received. Later, when the cards arrived, I checked my records and delivered the number of boxes each family had ordered. I made additional college money that way for two Christmas seasons.

BOB AND DAD'S GARDEN

Every spring, it was my job to dig up our large garden. This, along with cutting wood, allowed for little leisure. After a period of days of digging, I used a hoe to break up the clods of dirt, and smoothed it off with a rake. Mom and Dad decided what to plant. Using a stick on the end of each row, Dad and I tied strings so that our rows would be straight. Planting was the most enjoyable part of gardening. I kept the garden watered, and when the plants and weeds came up, hoed the weeds. In time the garden yielded a rich harvest.

In our yard between the parsonage and the church were large cherry trees. In the fall—well—leaves fall. It was my task not only to cut the lawn, but also to rake up the leaves, collect them in a big basket, and distribute them over our garden plot. During the fall, winter, and spring the rains soaked the nutrients from the leaves into the soil.

BOEING BOUND

My last full-time job while in Burien was at Boeing Aircraft Company. My sixteenth birthday in mid May qualified me for a summer job, and I applied before school was out, and no resume was needed. Soon, I received word that I was hired for the summer.

Boeing produced several B-17 "flying fortress" bombers each day. Many of the plane's parts were manufactured by sub-contractors, and at the big plant, we put the planes and engines together. They were to meet the needs of both the American and British air forces since they were sustaining losses with planes being shot down in the war.

The shop I worked in produced three wing sections on our shift. I worked the mid-afternoon and evening "swing shift." The effects of the Great Depression were not completely over until after the end of the World War II. I worked eight hours of manual labor for 62 ½ cents per hour, which translates to exactly five dollars a day. I received less in eight hours than the current $7.25 federal minimum wage for one hour.

I put away the money I earned that summer for college. My goal was to save enough for one full year of tuition and room and board at college. Happily, I reached my goal. My

Dad's income was just enough to get by on, so I knew there was no way my folks could help me. I managed to complete college without a penny of debt with no financial help from my parents.

My Boeing job was bucking rivets—icebox rivets. The three wing units we put together each night involved the landing gear opening. Someone bored holes through the fuselage and the landing gear patch that was in place to strengthen it from the stress of the landing gear going up and down. Because it needed special strength, the rivets needed to be frozen when installed, so they were packed in ice. I climbed inside the wing, the riveter inserted a rivet, and I took my L-shaped bar and leaned against the rivet. When the riveter turned on his hammer machine, I would flatten the rivet to the surface. We did hundreds of these for each of the three sections during each shift.

The sound of the hammering machine on the metal wing surface was deafening. I put cotton in my ears, but that was not good enough. I now can boast of my "war injury" in terms of poor hearing in my left ear that was closest to the rivets. The rivet machine sounded like a machine gun.

One night, I was bucking rivets on the first wing jig, as we called it, when I was called out of the cramped wing. My boss apologized, saying that a woman was working with a man who had horrific body odor. He said for one night only we would change places. Yuk a'mighty! The body odor of that guy was piercing. I was out of the wing working close to him on a machine, and felt like I was going to vomit. Being that near him, I felt I was beginning to soak up his rotten odor. They must have instructed the man to bathe and use deodorant because it didn't happen again.

When we earlier lived in Olympia, my brother, Ed, worked on a farm during the harvesting of a hay field. He received one dollar each day for working from sun up to sun down in the summer heat. I didn't think I was doing too badly making five dollars a day. Not for that time in our nation's economic history.

A COMPELLING COMMITMENT

In August of the summer when I was either 13 or 14, our family went to annual conference and family camp at our conference camp ground. As I mentioned earlier, I had accepted the Lord as my Savior when I was a young child. I knew then what I was doing, and had tried to live according to what I knew was right. A child's decision is at one level, but now I was a young teen and approached spiritual matters from a more mature perspective. At this family camp, I made a deeper commitment to the Lord at my teen level of understanding.

On the last Sunday morning, the speaker used an allegory in his sermon. He began with the Israelites going into the Promised Land and settling into their new territory. Each family was allotted several acres of land on which to build a home and grow crops. He made an interesting correlation. Each piece of land was surveyed and the owner drove stakes at the four corners of his land. He spiritualized this by saying that Christians need to make a commitment by symbolically driving a stake to achieve spiritual stability. I realized that though I had accepted the Lord much earlier, I now needed to go deeper in my spiritual life. In response to his message, I went forward to the altar and made that deeper commitment to the Lord I knew I needed.

COMMITMENT TESTED

I was part of the youth group that sponsored activities during the family camp. Lots of kids had a girlfriend or boyfriend for the camp period. One girl took a shine to me and sent messages through other kids that she liked me, but I wasn't ready yet to pair off with a girl. I treated her with respect, but did not go any further than that. At the end of summer, school started. This girl, we'll call her Martha, lived in another suburb of Seattle. I had a surprise in store for me when Martha arranged to change school districts and attend Highline High School. A boy told me on the school ground that she had changed schools so she could be my girlfriend.

She was part of a group that met on one part of the school grounds during noon recess. I spent recess playing handball, a game much like racket ball, only we hit a small rubber ball against the wall of a building with our hands. One noon this same fellow came to me with a message. "Man, you're crazy! Martha came to Highline to be your girlfriend, and she also wants to be your lover. Man, you have it made. Join our group and be her boyfriend and you'll get anything you want from her."

I remembered the commitment I had made at family camp and realized that right then was a test as to whether I really meant that. With God's help, I resisted the temptation.

ANOTHER TEST

One noon one of the fellows I played handball with took me aside. He knew I lived one street over from the school and walked each way. He had an offer for me. My friend asked me what I thought about Judy, likely the most popular girl in school, who was beautiful and sexy. He asked if I had ever had sex with a girl, and I said no. "Wow, are you in luck! Judy lives a couple of blocks from you. Her folks both work, and after school she has the house to herself. She enjoys initiating boys with their first sexual experience. All you have to do is tell me and I'll work it out for you."

My commitment was being tested again. Once more, by the grace of God I was enabled to resist the temptation.

HOME ALONE

My sister, Lilian, was married, and her husband, Keith, worked in the shipyard as an electrician. He rode a ferry from Seattle to Bremerton where ships for naval warfare were built. They weren't satisfied with their apartment, and were looking for a better place to live. Conveniently, the people next door to us, across the lot where we gardened, moved out. Mom called Lilian and told her they could move in next door if they wanted to. They checked out the place and liked it. How lucky we were. My sweet sister was living next door.

Meanwhile, my brother, Ed, fell in love with Mable Lund. They both worked at Boeing. Ed was a production illustrator, making drawings of how to put complicated parts together in the airplanes, while Mable worked in an office and supervised quite a few secretaries. Ed proposed, asked me to be his best man, and the wedding was held. Now, Ed was gone from home. However, he and Mable rented a house down the street from us, so they were still in the same neighborhood.

Two weeks later, my other sister, Irene, was married right out of high school to Al Ekkens. Al was a budding young preacher, and they made a great pair. He preached and they sang beautiful duets. Our house became very quiet since I was the only one left out of a brood of four.

DAD'S WONDERFUL GIFT

When I was about to begin my sophomore year in Highline High School, Dad came up with an astonishing proposition. "Son, I love to hear you play the piano. You have an excellent touch. I want you to have piano lessons again, and with the best teacher available." He told me he had arranged with the high school for me to leave early one afternoon each week to go downtown and to Seattle Pacific College. That sounded frightening, but the best was yet to come. Dad said my piano professor would be Dr. John Hopper, the pianist of the Seattle Symphony Orchestra.

"Oh, Dad, I'm not good enough to take from a teacher like him! I've only had a couple of years of piano lessons."

"It's not a matter of where you are now, but where your teacher can take you. He's the best teacher in Seattle, and I want you to learn from him."

The day of my first lesson, I was filled with apprehension. I took the bus down town and another one to the campus of Seattle Pacific College, now Seattle Pacific University. There I found my way to the studio of John Hopper.

He welcomed me warmly and put me at ease as much as possible. First we talked, then he asked me to play a song from memory. I made it a practice to memorize everything I played, so we got off to a pretty good start. He gave me assignments for the next week and I retraced my bus route home. Dr. Hopper turned out to be not only a master musician, but also a master teacher.

One time he assigned a Chopin prelude that was only two lines long. It was beautiful and I put myself into it. During my next lesson we spent the entire time with him coaching me on playing that short piece. At one point he said, "Don't hit the keys; play into them like you are playing an organ." He held his hands over mine so I could not raise my hands and hit the keys. That day he taught me to caress the keys in playing that beautiful music.

Toward the end of my sophomore year, Dr. Hopper laid his hand on my shoulder and said, "Bob, let's talk." He told me that if I was willing to work hard and apply myself, I could have a successful career in music. He knew I was composing music on my own and encouraged me. That was heady stuff for a fifteen year old to hear from such a prestigious musician. I began to build my dreams for the future. I determined that my career would include composing music, piano performance, and training to become a music professor in a Christian college.

I planned to study piano with Dr. Hopper during my junior and senior years, then enter Seattle Pacific College and major in music. Following that, I planned to earn advanced degrees at the University of Washington. Hopefully, I would land a job as a music professor at a Christian college, preferably Seattle Pacific College. I laid awake some nights listening in my imagination to symphonies playing familiar hymns. One thing I wanted to do was orchestrate the music of hymns, which had not been done up to that time. Later, it was pioneered by Bill Peterson, Kurt Kaiser, and other Christian music artists.

In May of my sophomore year I turned 16 and arranged with Boeing to work during the summer. I told Dr. Hopper I would not be able to take lessons during summer months. He replied that he did not teach during the summer, but urged me to come back in the fall. I promised him I would—a promise I would not be able to keep.

BETRAYAL

That summer was again time for annual conference when the stationing committee and bishop appointed pastors to churches. We had been in Burien only three years. That year our denomination allowed churches to take a vote on whether the congregation wished their current pastor to return, which was only advisory. The vote in our church was almost unanimous in favor of my father returning another year. Mr. August Sternberg, the delegate to annual conference, reported to the district superintendent and the stationing committee that the church wanted my father to continue as the Burien pastor. However, two young married men in the church took exception to the vote. During annual conference they got the ear of our district superintendent. Unfortunately, he listened to those two guys rather than the vote of the congregation.

I worked at Boeing that summer, but had Saturdays off. The appointments of pastors were always read by the presiding bishop Saturday afternoon at the close of the annual conference. Saturday morning I rode a bus downtown, then positioned myself to hitchhike going north to Burlington. This was a safe and common practice in those days. I was fortunate, and by afternoon had gotten rides to take me to my desired destination.

After walking across the campus of the campground, I came to the central pavilion where the annual conference business meetings were conducted. I slipped in from the back and found a place to sit. I wanted to hear the report of the bishop. Dad was secretary of the conference and sat on the platform keeping a record of everything that transpired. He had an assistant, and I saw Dad leave the platform and go outside. He had seen me come in, and soon came in the back door to where I was sitting and motioned for me to come outside. Little did I know what he was about to tell me. I knew nothing about the two men who had talked to the district superintendent.

Dad came right to the point. "We are going to be moved," he said, "but I don't know where we will go next."

"But why?" I agonized.

Dad told me about the two men and their mission. He even told me their names. I was shocked. They were close friends of mine. One of them was my mentor who had taken me under his wing and scheduled me to play piano occasionally for church services. Emotionally, I felt torn. I had a plan for my life, and these men were disrupting it. I could hardly listen when the bishop stood up to read the appointments, but I did want to know where we would be going next. It turned out to be the city of Tacoma.

Back home, we prepared to move. A farewell dinner was held to say good-bye to us, and on that occasion, the two men who had betrayed my father came to me and told me they were very sorry I was moving away. I was stunned at their hypocrisy. I got away from them and hurried outside, where behind bushes I cried my heart out. I didn't want anyone to see me cry. After all, I was sixteen.

Fast forward thirty years. I was serving as an executive in the missions department of our denominational headquarters. Frequently someone needed to drive to South Bend, Indiana, or Fort Wayne to meet people arriving on a plane. I was asked to drive to South Bend to meet a new member of our denominational Board of Administration. When I learned his name, I slumped in my chair. He was one of those men who betrayed my father in Burien now coming to represent the churches in the state of Washington. On the way to the airport, I did business with God. I made sure I had forgiven the man for what he did. When I met him at the airport, he greeted me as an old friend, and I did the same.

All that aside, I'll have to admit that when we moved to Tacoma, I was one heartbroken kid.

CHAPTER SIX:
Facing the Future

Bob (right front) with the Tacoma church youth group

Homework done

Bob as a high school senior

*"Don't let anyone look down on you
because you are young,
but set an example for the believers
in speech, in life, in love,
in faith and in purity."*
(1Timothy 4:12)

OFF TO A BAD START

W hen I moved with my parents from Burien to Tacoma, I was one defeated kid. I had planned to study piano during each school year with Dr. Hopper, work summers at Boeing, and graduate from Highline High School. Now, I was leaving all that behind.

We moved in August and school started the day after Labor Day, so we were hardly settled into our next parsonage when I started school. We lived in the district of Lincoln High School, which was quite a few blocks directly south of us. Each morning I used my thumb to hitchhike to school in a time when it was safe to do that. Most days someone gave me a ride, but on occasion, no one stopped and I ran as fast as I could to get to school on time. Lincoln included sophomore through senior years. I enrolled as a junior and didn't know anyone in my grade level, and it took a while to develop friends.

Every day after school, Mom asked me to play the piano. "You haven't played since we moved," she said. I was so downhearted about the move that I had no desire to play the piano. I always made an excuse for not playing. Mom spoke to Dad. "Bob never plays the piano any more. We need to get him a new teacher." So Dad inquired from people he had become acquainted with and was told that the best musician in Tacoma was the organist at the First Baptist Church downtown. He was also an accomplished pianist.

Dad arranged for me to study piano with a musician recommended to him as the best piano teacher in the city. After school, I went downtown to the church, took my lesson, then rode a bus out to where we lived. I have no question that the teacher may have been the best organist and pianist in town, but he was a lousy teacher. He couldn't compare with Dr. John Hopper. After two lessons, I dropped out, which was a disappointment to Mom and Dad.

FILLING THE VACUUM

A huge vacuum existed in my life. I had few friends and no sense of purpose. I felt like the two years in Tacoma would be a parenthesis between my sophomore year and going to college. I still planned to attend Seattle Pacific College when I graduated from high school and major in music. But at that time, I was like a wandering star in the sky. I had no idea what was about to take place.

My situation began to change. In September our church's youth group elected officers. Since I was new, I figured I'd not be selected for anything. To my surprise, I was elected vice president. Soon I learned that being president was a figurehead position. The vice president was responsible for all the programs for our weekly Sunday evening youth meetings. Since we had no youth pastor, I was on the spot.

At first, I struggled with this responsibility. Gradually I persuaded other members of the group to lead meetings, while I planned others myself. Also, I was the only member of the group who knew how to play the piano, so I asked one of the girls to lead the singing. We sang various choruses. I memorized each one, and when someone suggested a new one, I had them hum the tune and picked it out on the piano while the person supplied the words. After a while, we had quite a repertoire of songs. It encouraged my parents when I came home from school and practiced the songs on the piano. Mom and Dad were delighted I was playing again.

CITYWIDE INVOLVEMENT

One of my new friends at school invited me to attend the Miracle Book Club downtown each Monday evening. I began taking the bus on Mondays to attend the interdenominational Bible studies. We sang choruses before the Bible study, and the leader was troubled because no one was willing to be the regular piano accompanist. When she pleaded for a volunteer to take over that role, I volunteered. I learned new choruses, which I in turn taught our church's youth group.

The Bible study leader decided we should have officers for the group, which numbered around 100. Unbelievably, I was elected president. The leader asked me to take charge of ten or fifteen minutes of the opening. This was another challenge. On occasion, I conducted officers' meetings before the club started and became friends with students from other schools. Also, I got to know quite a few other kids in the group.

At an officers' meeting, someone suggested the possibility of starting a Bible study during the noon hour at Lincoln High School. With advice from our Bible teacher, we made arrangements to do that. Mrs. Olson, a lovely Christian teacher, allowed us to use her classroom during first lunch, which was 30 minutes. We made similar arrangements for second lunch. I ate during first lunch, and when we elected officers for the group, once again I was chosen to lead. We had between twenty and thirty students in our group. We ate our bagged lunches while we carried on our Bible studies. We took turns leading a short devotional.

At the Miracle Book Club, the word spread about our Lincoln Bible club. Kids from other schools asked for help. A group of three or four of us took a bus after school to our cross-town rival, Stadium High School. The two schools always played each other in football each Thanksgiving Day as arch rivals. We swallowed our pride, went to the school, and advised a small group on how to start a student-led

Bible study. We also did this for a couple of junior high schools.

DISTRICT YOUTH LEADER

The superintendent of the Seattle-Tacoma District of our annual conference lived in Tacoma. Sometimes he and my Dad met and talked. Dad happened to mention to him how involved I was becoming in youth activities. The superintendent had begun monthly district-wide meetings on the first Friday evening of each month, which rotated from one church to another. The superintendent was in charge of planning each meeting. He said to Dad, "I've been thinking we ought to have a youth gathering before the adult meeting each month, but I knew of no one to head it up. I think I'll ask Bob if he will take it over."

Dad mentioned this to me, and one afternoon after school the superintendent visited our house. He told me he had in mind my being responsible to arrange each month for a speaker, song leader, special music, and a pianist. I was to serve as master of ceremonies for the gathering. In my other leadership positions, I drew from each group those to participate, but this sounded staggering. I expressed my doubts, and the superintendent asked me to pray about it. He wanted very much for me to accept the challenge.

At first, it seemed like too much, but after praying about it, I felt God wanted me to do it, so I contacted the superintendent and agreed to accept his invitation. In his advertising that went out to the churches each month, he included news about the youth meeting. Dad was a big help to me, for he knew the pastors and some of the lay people in the churches who could help me in various roles. I managed to come up with a program each month, but it wasn't easy.

MY CAR ACCIDENT

One Saturday evening, our youth group practiced for a Christmas program to perform for the church. We carefully selected the drama we thought was best and rehearsed every Saturday evening. That night after play-practice, I was taking home a few of the group in Dad's car. He was generous in allowing me to use the car.

I was driving along on a divided boulevard with a gravel surface. I was going the speed limit when suddenly I saw a car approaching rapidly from the left on a cross street. Neither of us had time to stop. I saw quickly that if I hit the gas pedal I might get across before the other car arrived at the intersection. It was unavoidable. I jerked the steering wheel to the right, then to the left to go around him. Just as I turned the steering wheel to the left, the other car hit the back of the left side of our car a glancing blow that didn't cause damage to the other car. However, that slight push was just enough to cause our car to turn sideways sliding down the gravel road. Before I could crank the steering wheel right again, the car fell over on its right side and skidded down the street making a horrible screeching noise.

People rushed out of their homes and helped us get out of the car. There were two of us in the front seat and three in back, including our youth advisor. When we were all out, everyone was able to stand, but our youth advisor's white hair was stringing down over her face. The worst part was that she had a cut on her face that was bleeding. In the dimness of the street light, she looked like a ghost. I was stricken with fear and grief. Later, the other fellow in the front seat told me I stood on his chest trying to open the car door above us to get out. I was so panic stricken I didn't realize I was doing that.

One of the neighbors called the police. Meanwhile, the other driver yelled at me asking why I didn't stop for the stop sign. "There isn't one," I said. "Yes there is!" We walked across the intersection, and there, behind a clump of bushes, was a stop sign, completely hidden from the view of passing drivers. When the police arrived, he asked who was at fault. I admitted that I had gone through a stop sign, but explained that it wasn't visible. However, he failed to put that part in his report.

I called my Dad and told him what happened. Since we owned only one car, he couldn't pick us up. He made some calls and friends came to assist us. The police called a tow truck to haul the car away from its resting place. On Monday, Dad called his insurance agent, who went to the scene and corroborated my claim that the stop sign was completely hidden behind bushes. He took pictures to prove his point. He told Dad that I should never have told the police it was my fault, since this could have been disputed using the photos. Because of the hidden sign, the city could have been held liable for the accident, but it was too late for that since I had confessed.

I told Dad I would never drive again. I didn't want to take that responsibility. A few days later when I returned home from school Dad said, "Bob, let's go downtown."

"What for?"

"You'll see."

We rode the bus downtown, then walked two or three blocks to an auto repair shop. My stomach was tied in knots as Dad checked out the car and pronounced it as good as it was before the accident. I wasn't prepared for what happened next. Dad reached out to hand me the keys to the car. I pulled back. "Dad, I'm never going to drive again!"

"Yes you are, and you're going to do it right now." Dad spoke those words with kindness in his voice, but he was firm. I had no choice but to obey my father.

I got behind the wheel, took a deep breath, and started the car. I backed it out carefully, then began driving gingerly down the street. "You don't have to drive so slowly," Dad said. I put a little more pressure on the gas pedal and drove home. When we got out of the car, Dad commended me. "See, you can drive safely. You always have been a careful and responsible driver. The accident wasn't your fault. You can always use the car when you need it if I don't have an appointment." His understanding and kindness still warm my heart.

ANOTHER RESPONSIBILITY

If I wasn't busy enough, the unbelievable happened. In the September Sunday School Board session at the beginning of my senior year, the board voted for me to teach the infamous boys class. The kids were ages six through thirteen. No one had been able to quiet the noisy group and teachers quit one after the other.

The first two Sundays were bedlam until I had an idea. I gave each boy a point for being present, one for bringing his Bible, and *two points for good behavior!* At the Christian Book Store I purchased sample prizes and placed them on a bulletin board with the number of points for each prize. At the end of class, I wrote down each boy's number of points for that day. When a kid acted up I'd say, "Okay, no good-behavior points for you today. Within two or three weeks, the boys were orderly and listened to the lessons. Nearby classes marveled at the quiet in the boys' class. The prizes counted up as the boys earned them.

Several boys were from church families, while the parents of others did not attend church. One week in preparing my lesson, I laid it aside and created my own lesson on how to become a Christian. I explained they could pray: *Lord, I am sorry for the things I've done wrong. Please come into my heart with your forgiveness and love and be my Savior.* The Lord will forgive you, come live in your heart, and give you the strength to live a good life. That Sunday morning the boys listened with rapt attention. At the end of the lesson, I asked if any would like to invite Jesus into their heart. Several raised their hands. I quickly reviewed what I had said and prayed with them. When I said Amen, they looked up with joy on their faces after they had accepted Jesus as their Savior.

One of the boys whose parents were not Christians was thirteen, four year younger than I was. He became a devoted Christian young man, and I arranged a scholarship for him to attend a Christian summer camp. Years passed before I discovered that when I graduated from Seattle Pacific College, Carl enrolled that fall. Four years later, when I graduated from theological seminary, Carl enrolled in that school as well. He followed my footsteps without my knowing it. Eighteen years later, I was a speaker at the Warm Beach Christian Camp in Washington State. One afternoon while I was standing on the lawn talking with a friend, I noticed a young man running in our direction. He threw his arms around me and gave me a big hug. "Do you remember me?"

"I'm trying to, you look familiar, but I can't recall who you are."

It was Carl. He was now married and an ordained minister pastoring a church, something I had also done. That day I realized the fruit of my teaching and mentoring with those once-rowdy boys. It turned out to be a wonderful pay day—the best kind!

SERVICEMEN'S CENTER

A minister, Rev. Bostrom, established a servicemen's center in downtown Tacoma for soldiers who came from nearby Fort Lewis into the city. The center was open Monday through Saturday with servicemen encouraged to attend church on Sunday. Whenever I had time, I rode a bus downtown and played games with the men—ping pong, pool, checkers, and other table games. Refreshments were available, and the men enjoyed interaction with teenagers.

On Saturday evenings, Rev. Bostrom conducted a service that was broadcast over a local radio station. He organized a servicemen's quartette and other music, as well as gospel preaching. Dozens of teens attended along with the men every Saturday night. It was our big night out for the week.

MY FIRST GIRLFRIEND
One Saturday evening, a curious arrangement was made. I had become fond of a girl at high school, and so had another guy. We had both tried to "go steady" with Betty, but she needed to decide which guy she preferred. Finally, she told a friend to inform us both to show up Saturday evening at the servicemen's center. She said we should each sit at the end of a row with room for one more. When she arrived, she would come and sit with the one of her choice.

I sat there nervous and hopeful, as did the other guy. Then it happened. Betty came in from the back of the room and sat by me. I was exhilarated! She was *my girl*. We dated throughout my senior year (her junior year). We always double dated with her sister and her boyfriend. We enjoyed being with each other, but we had a platonic relationship and never talked about the future.

During my senior year I worked afternoons and Saturdays at a department store downtown. There I met a friend of Betty's who worked at the store. When she learned my name, she exclaimed, "So you're the guy who's going to marry Betty!"

"What?"

"She told me you're going to college next year, and when she graduates from high school you're going to be married."

That was news to me. Marriage wasn't on the horizon in my thoughts, so as delicately as possible I ended our relationship.

SINGING FOR THE TROOPS
During Christmas vacation of my senior year, I worked full time downtown. One day my supervisor said the school office had called and asked that I be allowed to go to the docks and sing for the troops on a ship coming back from the war in the Pacific. I went to the dock and linked up with our choir director, along with other students. She told us the troop ship was quarantined because measles had broken out

on board. They had arrived in port, but could not get off the ship to join their families at that Christmas time.

Our choir stood on the dock and sang Christmas carols to the men who lined the edge of the ship. They whistled at the girls between songs, and everyone laughed at that. Our choir director asked if those of us who had previously contracted measles were willing to go aboard and sing to the men in the sick bay. I came down with measles twice, so I knew I was safe. When we sang to the soldiers in the sick bay, some of them cried. The songs reminded them of their homes and families.

A DRUNK INDIAN

During the two summers after my junior and senior years in high school, I worked full time in the night shift at a fruit and produce warehouse. Since I started work late in the evening, I frequently went downtown early to assist at the mission on "skid row," the area where alcoholics and the homeless spent their days and nights. I stood out on the sidewalk as mostly men staggered by, handing them gospel tracts and inviting them into the mission. I told them they could have a meal after listening to a gospel message. Several went in while others did not.

One night a few very drunk men staggered toward me. When I handed them tracts and invited them in, one responded. He was so intoxicated he could hardly stand or hold his head up. I took his arm and helped him in and sat beside him. He smelled strongly of cheap liquor, and I prayed that somehow the message would get through to him.

During the service we sang, then the speaker presented a simple gospel message. I noticed that tears were coursing down my guest's cheeks. When the speaker invited anyone who wanted to accept Jesus as Savior to go to the prayer room, I asked if he would like to go there, and he said he would. What this man confessed to me was almost unbelievable. He was an American Indian from a logging camp. He told me he was raised by a godly mother, and that he knew all about faith in Jesus. He admitted he had never accepted the Lord as his Savior.

He insisted God could not forgive his sins. I replied that Jesus died on the cross for all our sins, but he believed his sin was too great for God to forgive. He told me he served in the Army during the war in the Pacific area, and his unit invaded several islands occupied by the Japanese. He said he grew to hate all Japanese people after thousands of servicemen died in the Pearl Harbor attack. On patrol, he and a fellow soldier captured a few Japanese soldiers. They were supposed to take them back to the camp where they detained war prisoners. He told me, "I despised the enemy so much I began shooting them. One man begged me in perfect English to spare his life. He said he graduated from an American university. My heart was filled with rage and I killed him along with the others. Now, you can see why God cannot forgive me."

What a spot for a teenager. I put my arm around the man and reassured him that God would forgive him because Jesus paid the penalty for his sins when he died on the cross. Finally, he began to pray and ask God to forgive him. When he opened his eyes, he was a new man—a sinner saved by grace. When we stood, I noticed he was as sober and steady as I was.

"I must return to camp," he said. "I come here every weekend to drink and forget my past. I cannot stay here. I need to go back to camp." I gave him a Bible and walked with him to the bus station. He had drunk up all his money, so I bought him a ticket back to his camp.

This remains one of the most memorable experiences of my life.

CHRISTMAS JOB

My first job in Tacoma was a Christmas vacation job during my junior year. I applied at J.C. Penney and was hired to work in men's clothing. One of the experienced salesmen took me under his wing and taught me how to relate to customers. If a man comes in and buys a pair of pants, suggest to him that we have great shirts and ties to match. If he buys shoes, show him our display of socks. And so on. Before the Christmas rush was over, I had learned the knack of salesmanship. My job ended after Christmas, because they didn't need the extra help any longer.

WORKING IN THE WAREHOUSE

My father knew a Christian businessman who owned and operated a fruit and produce warehouse. Dad asked him if he could use some summer help, and he said yes. They needed more help in the summer during the growing season. I went to work late in the evening and slept during the day. I hated the schedule, but enjoyed the job. In late evening, farmers brought in truckloads of fresh fruit and vegetables, and I helped unload the trucks as they came in.

My main job was to prepare the "short orders" requested by the grocery stores that would be trucked to them in the morning. For example, one store ordered a crate of lettuce, while another ordered half a crate or one-fourth. My job was to put together an assortment of the smaller amounts in boxes for each store. In early morning, I helped load the trucks for delivery to the stores in reverse order with the last order loaded being the first to be delivered.

Some mornings as the sun was about to come over the horizon, the red glow of the rising sun turned snow-covered Mount Rainier into what looked like a strawberry ice cream cone. It was breathtaking. Each morning, I took the bus home, ate breakfast, and tried to sleep during the warm summer day. I don't think I averaged more than five hours of uncomfortable sleep each day with all the noises of the main street nearby and children playing in nearby yards screaming and yelling. But I managed to survive.

MY SENIOR YEAR AT WORK

During my first three years of high school, I crammed in as many classes as I could take, sometimes eliminating study halls. Thus, by the time I was a senior, my class load was much lighter. I applied downtown for jobs at various businesses and was hired by a department store. I obtained permission from the principal to leave early and go downtown to my job. I also worked all day Saturdays.

My assignment was in the baby department assembling cribs, strollers, play pens, and numerous other items. When stock became low, I brought boxes from the warehouse to our back room, assembled the furniture, then placed them in the sales department. One of the nice parts of my job was refilling the Coke machine every afternoon and on Saturday. My boss said, "I know you will be tempted to take a bottle, so I'm going to give you the privilege of drinking a cold one every time you fill the machine. That's how I became a Coke fan. During my years of working part and full time, I saved money for college.

SOMETHING WAS HAPPENING

Although I didn't realize it, something was happening in my life. At age 15, I had determined that my lifetime career was to be in music. I still held on to that goal at the age of seventeen when I was a senior in high school. What I did not comprehend at the time was that being thrust into places of spiritual leadership during those two years in Tacoma was shaping my life in ways unknown to me.

My plans were still clear. After graduation, I intended to enter Seattle Pacific College as a music major, study piano under Dr. John Hopper, then enroll in the University of Washington and earn advanced degrees that would qualify me to teach music in a Christian college. I admired the music professors at Seattle Pacific College, and wanted to follow the path they had taken. Or so I thought.

THE BLANK CHECK

One Sunday morning in church my father preached a sermon on doing the will of God. At the conclusion of his sermon, he invited members of the congregation to give God a blank check representing their lives. He said, "Imagine that you have a check in your hand. First, in your heart write in today's date. Then on the line where it says 'Pay to the order of,' write in the name of Jesus. Don't put anything where it calls for the amount, then in your heart sign your name at the bottom. In other words, give God a blank check to fill in whatever he wants to do with your life."

It was an intriguing idea, one that resonated with me. I went forward with others and knelt at the altar. In my heart I told God he could do whatever he wanted with my life. Of course, I was sure I knew what that was—to be a music professor at a Christian college. Yet, I realized that if God had other plans for me, this was a commitment to follow his will.

QUIET AWARENESS

Two or three Sundays later, following Sunday dinner, while in my bedroom upstairs, my Dad's morning sermon was running through my mind. I laid on my bed thinking about the truths from the Bible he had presented. I began to pray silently. My spirit seemed to be in tune with God's Spirit as I lay there. Then came a moment that changed my life. It was as if someone came into my room, flipped a switch, and turned on the overhead light. Suddenly, I understood God's will for my life. The Spirit of God witnessed to my spirit that he wanted me to enter the ministry.

This was a very biblical happening. The Bible says in Romans 8:16, "The Spirit himself testifies with our spirit that we are God's children." This is how we have the inner assurance, after we accept Jesus as our Savior, that we are in a right relationship with him. On this momentous afternoon in my life, the Holy Spirit silently testified to my spirit that he wanted me to enter the ministry. Immediately my thoughts went to the blank check when I committed my life to whatever purpose God had for me. This was my call to the ministry. It wasn't dramatic; it was quiet and a natural outcome of my relationship with God. I immediately surrendered to the Lord my plans for a career in music, and told him I would obey his will to enter the ministry.

What I did not know then was that being in the ministry would involve various chapters in my life. First, I served churches as a pastor. Then, with my little family, we ventured to the Philippines as missionaries. While heading the Light and Life Bible College, I taught a full load of classes. One day the thought came to me, *your dream was to be a music professor in a Christian college. Look at what you are doing.* I was amazed and delighted. I was teaching two music courses and teaching keyboard to eight students who were preparing for the ministry. My dream was being fulfilled.

Following those years, I was asked to fill the role of a missions executive in the home office. Next, my church leaders asked me to serve as editor of our denominational magazine, which I did for almost ten years. Following that came another chapter as book editor for our denominational publishing house. My last formal role was on the pastoral staff of a church in Indianapolis for four years, closing out fifty years in the ministry.

I could never have planned my life like that. But when I turned my life over to God to fulfill his will, he opened doors for me to minister in ways I never could have imagined. It all began with the quiet awareness of the Spirit of God speaking to my spirit that he had plans for my life. I didn't know then what was ahead for me, but I'm glad I yielded my will to God's will. He has done a much better job of planning and managing my life than I could have done on my own.

BREAKING INTO PRINT

I was deep in thought about God and my life when the idea came to me that I had an ideal in mind for what kind of man I wanted to grow into. On an impulse, I took pen and paper and wrote a short poem called "My Ideal." Later, I showed my poem to Dad, and he asked if he could have it long enough to type off a copy. I agreed, and Dad made his copy. Weeks passed until one day when I arrived home from school Dad said to me, "Bob, take a look at our denominational magazine that came today." I always did look through it when it came, and I sat down and began to page through it, reading the things that grabbed my interest.

I turned a page, and to my great surprise there in the center of the page in a box was my poem. Dad had sent it in to the editor, a man whom I greatly admired. Little did I know at age 17 that one day I would become editor of that magazine. The poem reads like this.

MY IDEAL
Perfection is like a rosebud
That yet has much to unfold;
Within its fragile, delicate form
Lie wonders too great to be told.
I want to be like a rosebud
And blossom out in God's plan;
To be in God's will and be perfectly still
Is my ideal of a man.

THE DEATH OF OUR PRESIDENT

The Second World War in Europe and the Pacific was winding down. In my junior year of high school a startling event happened. I remember with pain what occurred on April 5, 1945.

Everyone in the school was in class when suddenly we heard the crackling sounds of the intercom loud speaker coming on, which was unusual during class hours. Our principal made the sad announcement that President Franklin Delano Roosevelt had died. He added that President Roosevelt's favorite song was the hymn, "Abide With Me." Next, we heard the recorded singing of that hymn over the intercom. We sat there stunned and deeply moved. Some of the students wiped tears from their eyes. To this day, every time I hear the hymn, "Abide With Me," it reminds me of President Roosevelt.

THE WARTIME DRAFT

With my 18th birthday approaching on May 13 of 1946, my last month in high school, I was faced with a serious decision. The wartime draft ended May 15. Normally I would have been drafted into the Army or voluntarily joined another branch of the armed services, but my principal had other ideas. He arranged well ahead of time with the draft board for all students whose eighteenth birthday came before May 15 to have a deferment until the end of the school year. However, the principal allowed military recruiters to come to the school and interview those of us who had received a deferment. My turn came in April when I sat down with an Army recruiter. He told me if I would sign up with the army before May 15, two things would happen.

First, he said that in the wartime draft law all solders received a free college education when their enlistment ended. I knew that to be true. But he went a step further. He told me if I enlisted for three years, I could choose wherever I wanted to go in the world after basic training. I didn't realize it at the time, but my father later told me it wasn't true. And it did turn out to be a lie. I went home from school and talked with my folks. "I can get a free education at Seattle Pacific College if I join the Army before May 15." Mom and Dad listened to my excited story, then Dad spoke.

"Bob, I want you to hear the other side of the story. I'm going to arrange to drive you to Seattle to meet with the president of Seattle Pacific College. Let's see what he has to say." Soon after, I obtained permission to leave school early one afternoon and Dad drove me from Tacoma to Seattle Pacific College, about an hour's drive. I was in awe as we were ushered into the office of the president, Dr. C. Hoyt Watson. He immediately put me at ease. He stepped from behind his desk, shook our hands, and invited us to sit down with him. He began by asking me about my plans after high school. I told him I planned to enter the ministry, then recounted my story about entering the Army and receiving a free education. Dr. Watson listened without interrupting me, then spoke.

"Bob, we keep records of young people who plan to come to college but decide to do something else first. Very few of them end up attending our school. Some get into a career path, while others marry, have children, and can't afford to come to college. As for the Army, it is true that you would receive an education if you chose to go on to college. But think about this. You would be subtracting three years from your ministry."

Then he made an offer. "Since your father called me, I had our office check with your school and discovered that you are in the top echelon of your graduating class. This qualifies you for a generous scholarship covering part of your expenses for two years." He went on. "Also, a work scholarship is available to help pay for your tuition, room and board. Some students work through the summer as well as during the school year. The chances are, with the savings your father told me you already have, you should be able to work your way through four years of college." I sat there hardly able to believe what I was hearing.

"Bob, you have to make your own decision. But I invite you to consider coming directly to college from high school. The choice is yours." Somehow, sitting with a college president at the age of 17 didn't seem so unreal after Dr. Watson so warmly welcomed and spoke with me. Dad stayed out of the conversation, and I told Dr. Watson I would pray about the matter and decide. He made sure I left with a packet of application papers to fill out and send in if I chose to come directly to college.

On the way home, Dad said nothing to influence my decision. He only asked me what my thinking was. I told him I was strongly considering going directly to college rather than joining the Army, and that ended up as my choice. At the graduation of my class of 710 students, I was one of those who received a scholarship handed to me with my diploma. My future was decided.

"IRON IN YOUR SOUL"

As I look back, I have deep gratitude to God for leading me in the ways he wanted me to go. I could not have planned my life nearly as well as it has developed over the decades with God in charge. I'm so glad that as a teenager, I turned over the leadership of my life to God. I am eternally grateful for his faithfulness in guiding me.

To close my story up to that point, I must tell you what happened the day I left for college. A friend of mine who was also going to Seattle Pacific College owned a car, and we arranged to travel together. He pulled up in front of our house and honked his horn. The moment of the beginning of the rest of my life had just arrived. I hugged and kissed Mom and Dad, then headed out the door with my suitcase in hand. I was grateful for the way they had raised me.

As I stood in the doorway, my mother uttered words that still echo in my mind and heart.

"Bob, I am praying that God will give you iron in your soul."

THE BEGINNING

CPSIA information can be obtained at www.ICGtesting.com
Printed in the USA
LVOW042248260312

274848LV00001B/26/P

9 781619 964693